Brand New Year: 52 Ways to Create a Distinctive Personal Brand

Donald P. Roy, Ph.D.

DEDICATION

To everyone striving to build their best personal brand.

— Don

CONTENTS

Introduction
Open for Business

As a college professor, I love the first day of a semester. This reset is a time of great anticipation and excitement. It is like New Year's Day. Many students embrace this new beginning with energy and optimism. However, the shine of newness soon fades and the grind of classes, assignments, exams, and other tasks can overtake the big picture goals of learning and personal growth.

The struggle to keep focused on goals is not limited to the journey of college students. We often become sidetracked while on the road to growth. It is not deliberate self-sabotage. Rather, losing focus tends to come from a combination of competing demands on our time and others making their priorities our problem. Our focus shifts from managing your situation to putting out other people's fires. The next thing you know, months have passed and we have not even begun that project or started working toward an important personal goal.

Always On

When it comes to managing your personal brand, you cannot afford to let competing priorities consume you. Why? Think about it, no one else in the world has as much motivation or urgency to care for your identity and reputation as you. Even the people who love you most— parents, significant others, or close friends— have less vested in your success.

What I am about to share with you is not meant to scare you; I merely state fact when I say once you embrace a personal branding mindset, you have made the decision to be "always on." Your brand is not active Monday-Friday 8:00-5:00 only.

A brand is an ongoing concern. Nike cannot afford to take a day off from caring for its identity, and neither can you. This call to be always on is not intended to be a burden. You will not be working at 3:00 a.m. (unless you choose to work at that hour). But, for best results you will always be mindful of how your values, thoughts, attitudes, and actions impact personal development and how you are perceived.

What Is It?

Before embarking on a year-long journey to build a better personal brand, it will be helpful to establish what we mean by personal branding. One of my wife's co-workers said she equated personal branding with tattoos that have names or symbols of loved ones. If you are averse to body ink no worries, personal branding does not require getting tattooed.

In the book *Me: How to Sell Who You Are, What You Do, and Why You Matter to the World*, Colby Jubenville and I define personal branding as "a process for identifying, developing, and communicating your unique value." The process of personal branding is the ongoing, always on approach to fine tuning and improving the unique value you offer.

How to Use This Book

Details on personal branding and suggestions for fulfilling the awesome responsibility of managing the world's most important brand appear in the pages that follow. You will find 52 ideas for implementing a personal brand mindset. Reflect on one idea each week over the next year and through on the Brand Builder recommended action at the end of each chapter. Some ideas will have significant positive impact on your brand. You will scoff at other ideas as being so not you. That sentiment is fine, but even if you feel that way about a particular idea reflect on how it could help build one's personal brand.

I am grateful for the opportunity to share personal branding ideas with you. *New Brand Year* is not written from the standpoint of an expert or teacher as much as it is written from the perspective of someone who is grappling with the same challenges as you to build a meaningful brand.

Let our year-long journey begin.

1
Yes, You Are a Brand
Take Charge of Brand You

Whether you like it or not, the first step you must take in managing your professional identity is to acknowledge that you are a brand. For some people, the idea of treating their career like brand managers manage the identity of Starbucks or Under Armour may be unsettling. After all, you are a person, not a product sitting on a shelf! But, if you do not embrace a brand management mindset you will be neglecting the most marketable asset you have: you.

Why You Must Be a Brand

Begin a new brand year by committing to managing your personal brand. The marketing definition of a brand is that it is a name, symbol, or other marks that distinguishes one seller from another. It is the latter part of the definition (distinguishes one seller from another), that makes it imperative for you to manage your career like a brand.

Consider three reasons why you must take control of your brand:

- *A brand must have a defined meaning.* Think about a brand you admire or that you connect with on an emotional level- it is likely that the brand resonates with you because of its values, priorities, or purpose for existing. Similarly, people will be attracted to you when they can relate to the core of your brand that defines you.

- *Differentiation is essential.* Most businesses avoid at all costs finding themselves in a situation known as Commodity

Hell. It is a term that refers to an inability to distinguish a business's offerings from other sellers (the definition of what a brand is meant to do). Differentiation must be real and relevant. You could dye your hair purple or wear polka dot clothing every day and be different, but the difference would not add value to other people. Personal brand differentiation occurs through not only a clearly defined meaning (i.e., purpose and values) but also an ongoing commitment to acquiring and strengthening skills that benefit others.

- *You have competition.* Differentiation would not be so important if the need to stand out was not so great. Competition exists to get a foot in the door to start your career, to move up in an organization, and to branch out into new opportunities. The good news for you is that most people do *not* manage themselves like a brand, thus making your quest to position your brand for success easier. The decision to manage your brand in itself does not guarantee success, but it puts you ahead of many would-be competitors.

Beware Personal Branding

You may have encountered the term personal branding before. It is an often misunderstood and incorrectly applied concept. Are the 51 ideas that you will read in this book relevant to personal branding? Yes, but the term will be used sparingly. Why? Too many definitions of personal branding are short-sighted. Specifically, they focus on image or communication such as your photo on LinkedIn or results that show up in a Google search of your name.

These attributes about you are important, but building a brand is so much more than outward appearance. You may have heard the expression "you can put lipstick on a pig, but it is still a pig." That idea applies to brand management, too. A slick website or stunning photo does not a brand make.

Communication of your brand is important, but it follows laying a solid foundation of meaning as well as acquiring skills and abilities that make up the value you have to offer an employer or clients. Your brand is made up of what we can call the 3Ms:

- *Meaning*. Purpose, passion, values, and goals that influence your decisions and actions.

- *Makeup*. Composition of your mindset toward how you create value and the skills you possess to deliver value.

- *Message*. Communication of your brand's meaning and makeup to persuade others about your value offering.

Adopting this three-dimensional view of your brand will help you make decisions on how to set priorities, what opportunities to pursue, and how to engage with other people.

Brand Builder

Begin your new brand year by embracing the possibilities managing your brand provides- gaining clarity of the meaning that defines you, establishing your unique value, and standing out from competition. You need not worry that you do not have the answers yet; your journey through this book will lead you to them.

2
Why Do You Wake Up?
Let Purpose Drive Brand Meaning

What makes a brand great? The tendency is to point to masterful branding like a sleek logo, distinctive product packaging, or memorable advertisements. Those tactics are just that- tactics that carry out a broader strategy. Truly great brands do not ascend to that status because of their marketing. They get there by having a clearly defined purpose that drives every decision made.

One of the best examples of a brand driven by purpose is Patagonia. The outdoor gear and clothing company founded by Yvon Chouinard in 1973 has built a reputation as a company focused on fulfilling its mission. Patagonia's mission is straightforward yet clearly states the company's reason for being:

Build the best product, cause no unnecessary harm, use business to inspire and implement solutions to the environmental crisis.

When your purpose is as clear as Patagonia's decisions about opportunities to pursue, establishing priorities, and how to allocate resources become less daunting to make.

Reason for Being

Before you turn attention to the tactics of building your brand, you have to understand the foundation upon which you are building. Defining purpose is not optional; you must be able to answer the question "What is my reason for being?"

Notice the Patagonia mission does not define its existence in short-term outcomes such as profits or market share. It is a statement of purpose about how Patagonia will create value for the world around it.

9

Finding Your Purpose

In order to find the answer to the purpose question of your reason for being, you need to know where to look. An ideal starting place is to recognize how values shape your purpose. Values are the principles that guide every decision you make. Like a compass, values give direction in making judgments about what is important (and unimportant), what is right (and wrong), and what brings you happiness (and unhappiness). Many instances of dissatisfaction or unhappiness with any life decision, including career choice, can usually be traced to a decision that does not align with one's values.

Identifying your values is not a straightforward process because values do not reside in one area of your life. In determining how values relate to your professional life, look to these four sources:

- *Intrinsic.* What activities or tasks do you engage in because of the enjoyment they bring?

- *Work content.* What specific roles or responsibilities do you enjoy taking on because they play to your strengths or skills?

- *Work environment.* What conditions are conducive to creating happiness and motivating you to perform to your abilities (e.g., company culture, growth opportunities, and compensation)?

- *Work relationships.* How important is interaction with others (e.g., collaboration and diversity)?

Understanding how these four sources of values impact your purpose will act as a filter to help you to identify opportunities that align with your purpose.

Brand Builder

Don't go another week into your brand new year without defining your purpose. Purpose lays your foundation. Another way to look at purpose is that it answers the question "Why do I wake up?"

Craft a purpose statement with these three elements:

- *Who am I?* Answer this question by identifying your aspirational profession or industry (it may or may not be where you are now), target market served, and type of work you do.

- *What do I do?* Think beyond job descriptions by recognizing how you create value for other people and why is it valuable to them.

- *What is my impact?* This question is the "so what" follow up to the "what do I do" question. Pinpoint the significance of the value you create.

Once you have answers to these three questions, write your own purpose statement, memorize it, make copies of it- do whatever it takes to keep it top of mind and live it. Here is a template to help you:

I, (your name), am (description of industry, occupation, market served, or job title) that (value created and benefit).

Keep it simple and let it be the measuring stick against which you evaluate every decision you make that affects your personal brand.

3
What Would You Do For Free?

Use Passion to Fuel Your Purpose

You will spend *a lot* of time working during your professional career. Assume a 40-hour work week (a traditional norm in the United States) for 50 weeks a year (hopefully you will have more than two weeks of vacation, but 50 hours is a round number for illustration purposes). Those estimates total 2,000 hours on the job annually and 90,000 hours over a career that spans from early 20s to mid-60s.

Calculating these figures on time spent at work is not intended to depress you but rather inspire you to think about choosing work that will bring joy and fulfillment to most of those 90,000 hours. The secret is to find a passion that can be related to a career.

Finding Your Passion

Passion is a word that conjures positive connotations. One definition of passion in the Merriam-Webster Dictionary is "intense, driving, or overmastering feeling or conviction." It would be a blessing to land a job in which you went to work each day and experienced passion as described here. But, finding your passion involves more than finding your "happy place."

Interestingly, the Latin origin of passion has little to do with joy or happiness. The word passion comes from the Latin "pati," which means "to suffer." Whoa! Most of us want to avoid suffering, not seek it out. A deeper interpretation of passion is that it is linked to something for which you are willing to invest heavily- time, effort, and yes, suffer through occasional adversity and disappointment. But, when you have an intense emotional connection you have with something for which you are passionate, you will endure adversity to enjoy the pleasure and satisfaction derived from the endeavor.

Recognize Your Passions... But Don't Follow Them

Perhaps the worst career advice given these days is "follow your passion." These three words are dangerous, even if they are well intentioned. The premise of this advice is when your passion becomes your work, it does not see like work. That state sounds like a place you want to aspire to reach, but will it challenge you? Will it make best use of your skills? Will it allow you to meet the financial and quality of life goals you have? Maybe... or maybe not.

Rather than searching for a way to turn a passion into a career, a different approach is to open yourself to your career fueling passion. Psychologist Cal Newport has researched the passion-career relationship extensively. Newport concludes that a pre-formed passion cannot be forced into a career, and that passion is earned by developing it through carrying out your purpose. In this view passion is developed, not followed.

Brand Builder

Passion is fuel flowing from purpose. Consider how you can create a brand that is energized by passion by doing the following:

- Identify a task (e.g., solving problems) or cause (e.g., teaching children to read) for which you are passionate. How closely does your answer relate to brand purpose established previously? If it is closely related, your passion potentially can be fulfilled through your work. If it is not closely related, the particular passion might be better pursued through hobbies or volunteerism.

- Ask the question "what work would I be willing to do for free?" (Assuming that basic needs are met). If your answer is based on doing work that carries out your purpose, it could be inspired by passion. If your answer is based on doing work that is easy or would not be too strenuous given you do it for free, it is likely not a passion.

- Focus your work (or pursuit of work) on opportunities that connect purpose and passion.
  - Purpose without passion= Going through the motions of life
  - Passion without purpose = Experiencing joy but not achieving deeper meaning.

The intersection of purpose and passion is the authentic you- personal meaning that is not manufactured or created to impress others.

4
A Balanced Scorecard
Set Goals to Fulfill Brand Meaning

Success in your career as well as other aspects of your life will be determined largely by meeting three conditions: 1) Know what you want to achieve, 2) develop an understanding of what it takes to get there, and 3) have an action plan of steps that must be taken along the journey to reach your goals.

Think of the three conditions, as ready, aim, fire. Having goals (ready) orients you to the outcomes you desire to experience. Understanding what it takes to get there (aim) equips you with knowledge of how you can make use of your strengths and which weaknesses must be shored up to align your abilities with your aspirations. An action plan (fire) is your map for getting from your current state to targeted outcomes.

It is early in your new brand year, and it is time to ensure you have gone through the ready, aim, fire steps to create goals that will give you direction.

The Multi-Dimensional Personal Brand

You are reading this book because you want to strengthen your personal brand, most likely for professional benefit. While achieving professional goals can lead to internal fulfillment and external rewards (e.g., raises and promotions), avoid becoming a one-dimensional brand. A complete personal brand is multi-layered, with your brand building quest taking you on a growth journey by setting six types of goals:

1. *Career.* Targeting organization with which you desire to work, job or duties, new skill development, and advancement plans.

2. *Relationship.* Seeking out a mentor (or someone to mentor), networking within your organization, expanding industry contacts, and developing mutually beneficial connections outside of business.

3. *Wellness.* Maintaining physical and mental well-being.

4. *Spiritual.* Using study, prayer, meditation, or reflection to understand and develop your purpose.

5. *Financial.* Making decisions regarding income, savings, debt reduction, investments, and discretionary purchases.

6. *Bucket List.* Allowing yourself to enjoy new experiences, including some experiences that could take you out of your comfort zone.

As you set goals in these six areas, realize that they will fall in different time horizons. Some goals may need to be pursued immediately (e.g., losing 10 pounds in the next 30 days) while others will be pursued over the course of the year (e.g., meditating for 20 minutes each morning).

Avoid a Dangerous Personal Branding Myth

A great deal of advice dispensed about personal branding is misguided because it equates personal branding with communication tactics. Yes, your social media image and content are important, and you benefit from having a professional appearance online via your website or blog.

The reason this mindset is a myth is that an obsession with the tactical requirements of self-marketing misses the point of building your brand: To create a holistic being that experiences fulfillment from living your purpose. This word of caution is given as a reminder that most personal branding experts do not relate their wisdom about self-branding to achieving growth that is balanced across different life roles. Plan for growth by setting goals in the six areas outlined to position yourself for career success and a life of fulfilled purpose.

Brand Builder

Tap the power of goals to give direction and chart a path to growth by doing the following:

- State outcomes you would like to experience across the six goal categories (career, relationship, wellness, spiritual, financial, and bucket list). Do not make any restrictions about the number of goals in a category or in total. The focus at this point is to put down everything you would like to be, do, or have in the next year.

- Once you have brainstormed for all categories, prioritize or rank your goals within each category (ideally you will have at least one goal in each of the six categories). Then, reduce your list to a smaller number of goals, identifying a "Top Six List" that contains the goal representing your top priority for growth over the next year. Your Top Six List should be considered your brand's strategic priorities.

5
Ready, Aim, Fire
Be SMART in Setting Goals

Success in your career as well as other aspects of your life will be determined largely by meeting three conditions: 1) Know what you want to achieve, 2) develop an understanding of what it takes to get there, and 3) have an action plan of steps that must be taken along the journey to reach your goals.

Think of the three conditions, as ready, aim, fire. Having goals (ready) orients you to the outcomes you desire to experience. Understanding what it takes to get there (aim) equips you with knowledge of how you can make use of your strengths and which weaknesses must be shored up to align your abilities with your aspirations. An action plan (fire) is your map for getting from your current state to targeted outcomes.

It is early in your new brand year, and it is time to ensure you have gone through the ready, aim, fire steps to create goals that will give you direction.

Why You Need Goals

The last chapter ("A Balanced Scorecard") made the case for considering what you want to accomplish across a variety of life roles, not just how you want your career to play out. Once you have pinpointed the outcomes you aspire to realize, the next task is to set a plan to get to the desired destination.

Goals serve as the plan to get from Point A to Point B. You would not decide to take a road trip from Chicago to Manchester, Tennessee (home of the Bonnaroo Music and Arts Festival) with no more of a plan of "drive south." Yet, many people set goals with little thought about how to achieve them. Having a goal is better than not having one- it is estimated that 80 percent of adults do not have written goals- but to enhance chances of goal achievement goals must meet certain criteria.

Avoid the Trap that Sinks Most Goals

Perhaps the best known type of goals are New Year resolutions. They are also the worst example of goals you can find. Why? Most New Year resolutions set us up for failure or at the very least, do not hold us accountable. The reason is most New Year resolutions are not properly set as goals.

For example, a New Year resolution to "exercise regularly" lacks specifics of how often. Also, it does not even define what "regularly" means. No wonder health clubs and gyms are packed in January only to find just the regular crowd coming in within a few weeks. Most New Year resolutions (and many other goals for that matter) sound more like a hope or wishful thinking rather than a goal to which we can commit to meeting.

The solution to the improperly set goal is to be SMART in your goal setting. SMART goals are:

- *Specific*. The desired outcome is clearly stated (add $1,000 to savings account).

- *Measurable*. Often, a specific goal makes it measurable so it can be determined whether a goal is achieved.

- *Achievable*. A goal should be able to be met. If you have never earned more than $40,000 a year, a jump to $1 million in the coming year may be out of reach. Goals should inspire action, not leave us dejected when we cannot attain them.

- *Realistic.* A realistic goal often goes hand-in-hand with an achievable goal. A 25-fold income increase in a year is not the norm.

- *Time-bound.* Set a date by which the goal should be met. A sense of urgency is created when performing against a clock (e.g., add $1,000 to savings account by December 31).

Setting SMART goals does not guarantee reaching the desired outcomes, but the process of setting and striving to meet goals creates opportunities to grow even if goals are not fully met. Or, as author and motivational speaker Zig Ziglar said, a goal properly set is partially achieved.

Brand Builder

Tap the power of goals to give direction and chart a path to growth by doing the following:

- Select the outcomes in the six goal categories (career, relationship, wellness, spiritual, financial, and bucket list) you believe would have the most impact on your growth and well-being, professionally and personally, in the next year (you should have a list developed already from the previous Brand Builder exercise). State as goals, applying the SMART technique for goal setting to create goals that will give you focus on prioritizing and spending time and energy.

6

Will the Real You
Please Stand Up

Let Your Authenticity Set You Apart

To Tell the Truth was a TV game show that had an incredible run, airing from 1956-1968, then enjoying revivals at different points in time between 1969 and 2001. The show featured a panel of celebrities that questioned three contestants. One of the contestants had an unusual occupation. The other two contestants answered questions as if they were the person with the unusual occupation. The celebrity panel attempted to tell which contestant was telling the truth. The climax of each episode occurred when the host said "will the real (person's name) please stand up."

Some contestants were very convincing in answering questions as if they were the target contestant. They were able to role play or pretend for a few minutes that they were someone else. A brand does not have that luxury. In an "always on" world when we are connected to one another at all times, there is no occasion in which being someone other than the real you is an advisable brand strategy.

The need to be the real you at all times is a call for brand authenticity. That term is used frequently in marketing, but what does it mean? More importantly, why should you be concerned about authenticity?

What Being Authentic Means

Having an authentic sounds important (and it is), but what does brand authenticity mean? Instead of a lone definition,

25

the following are some different takes on the meaning of authenticity:

- Being conversational in words, visuals and other communication forms

- Celebrating being real, which means being honest, to the point, unapologetic, and sometimes, edgy

- Staying true to who you are, what you do, and who you serve

- Transparency in all dealings, from what you say on social media to a willingness to share what is going on behind the scenes

- Presenting who you really are and what you truly believe.

A misconception about brands is that the ultimate goal is perfection in which missteps or failures do not occur. Good luck with that! Rather than striving for an ideal that can never be attained, focus on authenticity instead of perfection. This choice includes the decision to allow vulnerability and imperfections to show rather than pretend they do not exist.

An Authenticity Check

How does authenticity fit with brand purpose and passion? Authenticity is the intersection of purpose and passion. You can recognize brand authenticity when you can articulate your meaning- why you matter to the world around you- and recognize the spark for your brand that is passion.

Understand that the pursuit of authenticity is not a project with a start and end date. Like branding itself, it is an ongoing journey. Your brand evolves and adapts to changes in the world around you—competition, societal values—as well as your own personal growth. For that reason, you will never "arrive" at having an authentic brand. Instead, you are on a never-ending pursuit to be real, honest, transparent, or other descriptors that you equate with authenticity.

Brand Builder

Author Oscar Wilde said "Be yourself. Everyone else is already taken." Although you will later read tips, suggestions, and best practices others have used to shape their personal brands, brand authenticity is a personal expression of how purpose and passion influence your actions.

Rather than striving to be the next Steve Jobs or Taylor Swift, embrace authenticity as an opportunity to stand out in your organization, industry and community. To work on that aim, do the following:

- Reflect on values and motivations that have been powerful influences on shaping your beliefs and behaviors.

- Based on values and motivation reflection, what words would you use to describe the "real you?" Would other people use these words to describe you? If yes, you likely are living your brand (i.e., being authentic). If no, a gap exists between how you perceive yourself and perceptions others hold about you, suggesting brand authenticity is lacking.

7
Breathe Life into Your Brand
Inject Personality to be More Relatable

For all of the similarities between marketing product brands and personal brands, one major difference is ever present: the role of personality traits in building brand image. Product brands have to manufacture personality to inject into their brands and hope that the market perceives them in the desired way. Marketing managers are tasked with breathing life into a nonliving entity.

You are a living entity. Better than that, you are a person with attributes and traits that make you interesting, unique, and valuable. In personal branding, the role of personality is not to create it but rather to reveal it. Your personality could be one of your greatest marketing assets, yet often it is masked or concealed in the quest to come off as "professional." Be professional, but be you at the same time.

Put the Person in Personal Branding

Do not mistake marketing yourself with creating a persona of someone who is not the real you. The goal of self-branding is not to project a perfect being that always says and does the right things. Rather, use your unique personal traits, regardless of level of perfection, to position yourself and convey the value you offer.

Technology is a great enabler of personal branding, but it can be a hindrance, too. For example, social media content distribution can be automated through services like Buffer or Hootsuite so that you can schedule posts at any time of day. But, if you rely too much on automated posts you miss out on opportunities to display a personal touch by interacting with others. Do not hide your personality behind a screen and keyboard.

Brand personality is a consistent set of traits to which people can relate. The good news about managing brand personality is just that- you can manage the traits people observe in you.

Use two tactics to make your brand personality distinct and reflective of you. First, answer the question "What do I want to be known for?" How you answer this question dictates the personality you reveal. Do you want to be seen as someone who is helpful? Friendly? Polarizing? Perceptions like these people hold about you are also personality associations held about your personal brand.

A second tactic for managing brand personality is to reveal your interests, thoughts, and opinions. This behind-the-curtain glimpse allows others to see you more as a person and less like an artificial being like product brands represent. What you share with others through social media posts, a blog, or your website can show your professional and personal interests. Photos, stories, links to articles or web pages, and quotes are examples of content that have been described as "personal hooks" that can shape how people view you as well as gain attention of strangers who are attracted to your personality.

You're not for Everyone

As you think about personalities you attract, you may realize that the personality you show the world will not appeal to everyone… and that is perfectly fine. Why? The goal of self-branding is not to create a universally beloved identity, for that is impossible. Instead, your goal is to leverage authenticity to create value for those to whom you matter.

Think about individuals whose careers are tied to their personalities such as actors, entertainers, and politicians. You may be turned off by Kanye West because you think he is arrogant. Another person will see Kanye's personality differently and will admire him. Same brand- two different responses.

Rather than engaging in a futile attempt to have mass appeal or not offend anyone, decide on which personality traits you possess are strengths you can use to attract and build a following and gain trust with people. This approach to letting your personality shape your brand is that it works for everyone. It does not matter if you are an extrovert or introvert, young or old; unknown or famous.

Get over trying to please everyone and use your strongest positive personality traits as a means to connect with other interested people.

Brand Builder

Now that you have been relieved of the pressure of trying to appeal to everyone, figure out how to use brand personality to your advantage. Reflect on the following questions:

- What personality traits of mine can I use to attract others to reveal my purpose, passion, and value?

- What do I want to be known for (i.e., distinctiveness)? What personality traits do I possess that will enable me to communicate distinctiveness of my personal brand?

8
Break the Chains of Assumed Constraint

Recognize the Threats that Limit Your Growth

Running is my favorite form of physical activity. It is my favorite not because I am fast or run long distances, for I can do neither. A morning run is an ideal start to my day because it is a time that I can allow my mind to wander or listen to a podcast (we will come back to podcasts later in your new brand year).

I have listened to hundreds of podcasts on my morning runs, but one message stands out above the rest. Motivational speaker and coach JB Glossinger encouraged his listeners to "break the chains of assumed constraint." In other words, do not allow self-limitations to keep you from overcoming obstacles that limit your growth and prosperity.

The timing of hearing that particular podcast could not have been better. A family vacation to Disney World was upcoming, and the stickiness of Glossinger's message enabled me to enjoy some of the rides that I would have avoided. I can vividly recall waiting our turn on the Tower of Terror at Disney's Hollywood Studios, saying to myself "break the chains of assumed constraint, break the chains of assumed constraint, break the chains…" until I stepped off the ride. Not only did I survive, but I enjoyed it!

Who Owns the Chains?

My experience at Disney World was the first of many occasions I have uttered "break the chains of assumed constraint" to get past self-imposed barriers to accomplishment. Although it is growth, what is most frustrating about these chains is realizing we are responsible for weighing ourselves down with them.

Most constraint is assumed; it does not actually exist. And in many cases, we have fitted ourselves with the chains that hold us back. Two self-talk questions explain why we engage in such destructive behavior:

1. *What if I fail?* Many of the goals you pursue require taking risk to get what you want. The risk may be real, such as investing your life savings in a business startup. Or, the risk may be psychological, such as worrying about what others will think about you if you do not achieve your goal.

2. *What if I succeed?* This reason for placing chains on ourselves may seem unlikely, but many people are worried that if are successful they will not know what steps to take next to sustain and build on their successes. This phenomenon may be an explanation for some "one hit wonders" in the music business. They did not know how to overcome self-doubt to create the second hit song.

Remember Shedding the Chains

The words of JB Glossinger have come in handy in the years since I embraced his message. Buying into the idea that most limitations we perceive are not real does not guarantee success. But, the choice to break the chains of assumed constraint and resulting benefits serve as reinforcements anytime self-doubt creeps in to "protect" you.

Consider some situations in which assumed constraint acts like a chain that limits your enjoyment or performance:

- *Meeting new people.* Are you a wallflower at networking events? Do you question why people would want to spend time talking with you? If your answer to these questions is "yes," you will be a wallflower and people will not want to spend time with you. And who is responsible for these outcomes? You will find the culprit if you look at a mirror.

- *Taking on a new project.* An invitation to join a project team could lead to building new skills, making new friendships, and receiving better job opportunities and assignments in the future. But, if you convince yourself that the risk exceeds the benefits or you are not up to the task, the chains of assumed constraint will keep you securely where you are.

- *Reaching for a breakthrough goal.* A few years ago, I thought about running a half-marathon. I had run a few 5K races, but I was unsure if I had 13.1 miles in me. The chains of assumed constraint were solid until I had a conversation with another runner who had run several marathons. He said he had watched me run and told me I could do it. I needed the encouragement of a fellow runner to break the chains and run the half-marathon, but I did it. Pursuing a breakthrough goal can make us feel vulnerable, so the weights of the chains appear to be more comfortable.

Brand Builder

You will not experience the opening of doors to new opportunities in your new brand year unless you leave behind the chains of assumed constraint. Remove the chains once and for all by answering the following:

- What causes you to own and drag around the chains of assumed constraint- fear of failure? Fear of success? Other worries? Knowing why you are saddled with the chains is the first step toward breaking free of them.

- Think of a situation in which the chains of assumed constraint affect your growth such as reluctance to engage in networking. What past successes allowed you to shed chains of assumed constraint? How can you transfer what you learned to deal with the self-doubt that is limiting your growth?

9
Success ≠ Happiness
Find Happiness While on the Success Journey

Several motivations can contribute to the driving force behind your quest for personal and professional growth. Among the motivations might be the belief of achieving success in one or more areas of your life will bring happiness. It stands to reason- if you achieve a higher level in your employer's organization, live in a desirable neighborhood, or have more money in your bank accounts you will be happier than if you did not have these things. But, the price of success must be paid to get there... or at least that is what the myth of success suggests.

The Myth of Success

You may be surprised to see the words "success" and "myth" used together. Success in itself is not a myth as it is a state you can attain. The myth is in the relationship between success and happiness. If the pursuit of happiness is the ultimate driver to become successful professionally, you can surrender today. Why? People who seek happiness have it backwards. German theologian and Nobel Peace Prize Winner Albert Schweitzer set the record straight on the success-happiness relationship:

"Success is not the key to happiness. Happiness is the key to success. If you love what you are doing you will be successful."

If you are looking for success to bring happiness in your life, you will likely come up empty and expend a great deal of effort in the process. Instead, make your quest one of finding happiness in who you are and what you do. Happiness is a precursor to success.

Finding Happiness

You have moved partially toward finding happiness already by taking time to understand your purpose identify your passion, and set goals. If you started reading this book expecting to get tips right away on how to improve your social media presence or how to rank higher in Google search results, you may have been disappointed. Those tactics are just that- tactics. They are not fundamental to the existence of your brand. Your brand foundation must be solid before building upon it.

Buying into the idea that happiness is the set up for success is one thing; figuring out how to see happiness in your life may be more challenging. Recognizing happiness requires you be observant of the successes and blessings you have had occur. Three times when you can reflect on happiness is at the beginning of the day, the end of the day, and throughout the day.

- *Beginning of the day.* Author and psychologist Dr. Wayne Dyer suggests using the first waking minutes of the day to reflect on everything in your life for which you are grateful. Doing so not only reminds you of the happiness you have already, it plants positive thoughts in your mind rather than dreading getting out of bed or worrying about the day ahead.

- *End of the day.* Some days, the trials and stresses of work, relationships, and finances leave you physically and emotionally drained. Many people find writing down their thoughts about the day in a journal or diary is a therapeutic release and an opportunity to remind themselves of all that is good in their life despite the stresses of the day.

- *During the day.* Reflecting on happiness in your life need not be relegated to the beginning and / or end of the day. You are presented with numerous opportunities to see happiness in your life as you go through the day. If you step outside to find a brilliant blue sky and comfortable temperature, a moment to be grateful presents itself. As you walk to lunch, recognize the gift of health that allows you to be at work and move about. When given a new project or challenge to complete for your boss, be thankful for the intellectual and creative abilities that put you in a position to be give the challenge.

In short, these three suggestions for recognizing happiness are calls to take time to smell the roses in your life.

Brand Builder

From this point forward, adopt the philosophy of Albert Schweitzer that happiness leads to success, not the other way around. Practice a happiness-first mindset by implementing the following practices:

- Use the beginning of day or end of day reflections (or both) to keep all of the sources of happiness in your life top-of-mind.

- Commit to living in the moment to appreciate all of the sources of happiness around you- friends, colleagues, nature, hobbies, and more- to appreciate the happiness that you have accrued already. And, it did not require "success" to receive.

10
Buyer Beware
Separate Personal Branding Fact from Fiction

Like it or not, you have a brand (I trust that you are at least receptive to the idea since you are reading this book). Many people do not perceive their professional identity as being like that of a product or corporate brand. Even some of the most conscientious, forward-thinking professionals might subscribe to the belief that their work speaks for itself. Self-branding is unnecessary as others will notice and recognize them as someone of value. In turn, payoffs will come in the form of extrinsic rewards such as promotions, bonuses, awards.

The scenario described above works—sometimes. Yes, others might notice the good work you perform and value created. Do you want to rely on the observation of others to realize what you have to offer? Proactive brand management is good practice. However, to be an effective brand steward you must understand up front what personal branding is… and is not.

Before wading deep into the personal branding waters, it will be useful to distinguish concepts from confusion. Sadly, there is quite a bit of misinformation about personal branding that contributes to ineffective practices. Let others engage in misguided self-marketing as you gain clarity on building your brand.

Straight Talk

My interest in personal branding is both professional and self-serving. As a college professor mentoring students, I tout personal branding as a strategy an early career professional can employ in making the transition from college to work. At the same time, I see a need to put personal branding concepts into action to manage my own professional identity. The more I research and observe personal branding practice and advice, the more frustrated I become. The frustration comes from the lack of understanding about what personal branding is... and is not.

Many people have not embraced personal branding because they are unconvinced it is for them. Sometimes, it is because they simply are unfamiliar with personal branding practices. In other cases, avoidance of personal branding is due to misconceptions about what it is and who benefits from it.

To get off the fence and into the game of building *your* brand, let's tackle five beliefs about personal branding that should not be accepted as truth:

- *Fiction: Personal brands are invented or created.*
  Fact: No, they cannot be contrived as they must be grounded in authenticity... the real you. A frequent branding misstep is that tangible attributes of branding (e.g., headshot, clothing, and website design) are often emphasized and elements central to who you are (e.g., values, motivation, skill set) are overlooked as major brand assets. The best advice is "be human." You are not trying to create an artificial being; you and your brand are inseparable.

- *Fiction: Personal branding is all about self-promotion.*
  Fact: Yes, communicating your value is a vital self-marketing action. However, it is a complementary piece to Meaning and Makeup- the primary sources of value you have. Audiences will soon tune out people who focus on promoting themselves without having a clear value proposition.

- *Fiction: Personal branding is a means to an end.*
  Fact: Personal branding *could* enhance your efforts to land a job, get into graduate school, or win an award. Taking such an approach to personal branding would deny you of its long-term payoffs. Rather than being a tactic to help you get what you want, personal branding is a strategy for living your professional life. It defines priorities, guides decisions on how to spend time, and inspires your work as value creation for others.

- *Fiction: Personal branding is not for introverts.*
  Fact: An authentic brand reflects one's true personality. If you are an introvert, you need not mask it. Instead, embrace it as part of your brand story.

- *Fiction: Having a brand is not important in my industry.*
  Fact: While the importance of personal branding might be greater in positions like consulting, freelancing, or selling, a brand carries influence in all professional settings.

Remember that when it comes to a brand, the owner must define the brand's meaning or those people who interact with the brand will define it. You decide who gets to define it.

Brand Builder

The saying "perception is reality" applies to personal branding. Your beliefs about what personal branding can or cannot accomplish in your professional life are fact, right or wrong. If you have bought into personal branding misconceptions, your brand building efforts could suffer.

Take personal branding myths you might be holding head-on by doing the following:

- Identify a negative personal branding belief you hold—it could be one of the five fiction statements mentioned previously or another belief you have that prevents you from enjoying the benefits of personal branding. Reflect on how you could change the negative belief so that it no longer works against your brand-building efforts.

- Create a positive statement, or affirmation, to dispel a personal branding myth you hold. For example, destroy "I am too shy to practice personal branding" with "I have clarity of brand Meaning and want to use it to create value to benefit others.

11
Soft and Proud of It
Soft Skills Set You Apart

If someone calls you "soft," the meaning associated with that label is often negative. Does it mean you are not strong? You are not forceful? You lack conviction? These traits are hardly a formula for professional success. However, another meaning of soft must be embraced to strengthen your skill set and enhance the value you offer to employers or clients.

When it comes to the skills required to perform your job, it is likely that among the most important skills are referred to as soft skills. They are self-management and people skills. Soft skills are difficult to teach in formal learning environments in the way that hard skills can be taught, and mastery of soft skills is more difficult to measure compared to hard skills. Yes, being soft is good for your career.

Why Soft Skills Matter

Employees and employers alike have identified gaps in soft skills development. This sentiment is not surprising if you consider that the emphasis of professional preparation, whether it occurs in a university, technical school, or on-the-job training, is hard skills instruction. Although having job-specific tasks is not optional in most professions, employers expect workers to possess another group of skills to manage themselves and interact with others.

Studies on skills needed in today's workplace have found the following skills are valued highly by employers:

- Communication

- Organizational

- Computer/Technology

- Interpersonal

- Analytical/Critical thinking

- Leadership

- Problem solving

- Time management

- Mathematical

- Professional

Only two of these ten skills (computer/technology and mathematical) are hard skills. The other eight skills complement one's technical or discipline training yet often do not get the same emphasis as hard skills in formal education and training settings.

Getting Better by Getting Soft

You may have heard the difference between hard skills and soft skills referred to as book sense versus common sense. While it is true that hard skills are learned through some means of instruction or "book learning," you should not rely on common sense alone for strengthening soft skills. Meet your need to strengthen soft skills by pursuing the following options:

- *Formal education.* Colleges and universities of all sizes ranging from the Harvard Negotiation Institute and Stanford University to local institutions offer negotiation courses and certificate programs.

- *Self-Directed Education.* Becoming more proficient at negotiation does not require you enroll in a higher education course or program. Websites such as Coursera and
  edX offer free courses taught through leading universities. Even more informal approaches to sharpening soft
  skills can be used such as reading books and blogs or
  listening to audio books and podcasts.

The learning resources are out there to build soft skills. You
must decide which ones best fit your learning style. Regardless
of which resources you use, the point is take advantage of them
to work on soft skills needed to make you more valuable to employers as you prepare.

Brand Builder

Soft skills not only complement formal education and training; they can make your professional value rise and create opportunities you may not have otherwise. Commit to enhancing
your soft skills by doing the following:

- Review the list of eight soft skills given earlier (communication, organizational, interpersonal, analytical/critical
  thinking, leadership, problem solving, time management, and professional). Identify one of these skills you
  would like to strengthen in your new brand year.

- Search formal and self-directed education sources related to the skill you seek to strengthen. Prepare a list of
  resources you will use (e.g., enrolling in a Coursera
  course, books to read, and blogs or podcasts to which
  you will subscribe) and get started. The list is useless
  without committing time daily or weekly to learn!

12
Hard versus Hardened Skills
Keep Your Toolbox Up To Date

Possessing soft skills can make you more marketable by having sharper self-management and interpersonal skills, but you will likely not be considered for a job if you lack the hard skills required to perform daily tasks. Hard skills are those skills that can be taught, their understanding and ability demonstrated, and performance measured. They are learned skills in which rules tend to stay the same regardless of company, circumstance, or co-workers.

Hard skills can be learned through formal education or self-directed learning. In order to make gains in personal brand equity, or value in your New Brand Year, you must set a baseline of hard skill capabilities and determine what hard skills need to be strengthened or learned.

Setting the Baseline

Every profession has a distinct set of hard skills, a blend of technical and business skills that are essential to perform competently. Use the following sources to gather information about the hard skills required for your chosen field:

- *Job postings.* A large number of postings across a wide range of fields can be found on career websites like Monster, CareerBuilder, and Glassdoor. Also, many industry-specific job websites exist that enable you to focus your search on jobs within that industry.

- *Social networking websites.* Think of social networking sites as virtual gathering places around interests, including careers. Use Twitter to create lists and follow hashtags related to career interests. Similarly, use LinkedIn to follow individuals and organizations in your field or industry. Connect with a community of professionals in your aspirational field using LinkedIn Groups.

- *Trade and professional organizations.* It is not uncommon for organizations competing in the same industry to join forces to promote their interests by forming a trade or professional association. The long-term health of any industry depends heavily on identifying and developing talented people who seek to obtain jobs in a field.

- *Practitioners.* Talk with someone who does that job. He or she will be able to inform you about the skill sets that you need to possess in that field or industry. Many professionals are ready and willing to help; it is a way of "paying it forward."

- *Teachers.* Tapping the wisdom of teachers or former teachers can be beneficial in two ways. One, most professors stay up-to-date about the hard skills employers seek from new hires. Two, many of them were practitioners prior to their teaching career. They have "been there, done that" and can give you a candid assessment of the skills that you need to build.

Use as many of these five sources you have at your disposal to gather information on hard skills needed to set a baseline for skill development.

Easy-to-Understand Hard Skills Development

The same two routes used to enhance soft skills can be used for hard skill development, too: Formal education and self-directed education.

- *Formal education.* Technical schools, community colleges, and universities are institutions people look to for training that will equip them with skills to compete in their chosen field. Two considerations for investing in formal education are curriculum and cost/benefit analysis. First, does the curriculum of an academic program include training in hard skills sought by employers? Second, the cost of a formal education must be weighed against benefits of building your hard skills set in terms of job opportunities, earning potential, and work-life balance.

- *Self-Directed Education.* Many options exist for a do-it-yourself approach to building hard skills, with the most popular ones being free online courses, skill-specific training, and public online resources. Free online courses today are packaged in what are known as massive open online courses, referred to in shorthand as MOOCs. These courses are offered by more than 100 universities in America including prestigious institutions such as Harvard, Stanford, and Vanderbilt.

Another source of self-directed learning materials is skill-specific learning platforms. Udemy offers some free courses with others costing anywhere from $9 to $499. Learners can complete courses at their own pace. Lynda is a subscription-based platform for online tutorials.

Finally, do not overlook the vast amount of free video and blogs on the Internet. A popular video platform for personal development is TED Talks. This collection of more than 1,800 videos is from the internationally known TED (Technology, Entertainment, and Design) conferences. TED speakers are generally known as leaders in their respective fields. Also, books and blogs are useful sources to keep abreast with what is going on in your field, including the hard skills required to succeed.

Self-directed education opportunities are so instrumental to your professional growth that they will appear several times in your New Brand Year journey.

Brand Builder

You have many options for acquiring and building hard skills. Regardless of how you do it keep this in mind: 60 percent of new jobs require skills that only 20 percent of workers currently have. Developing hard skills is a never ending project. With this challenge in mind:

- Compile a list of hard skills (i.e., knowledge, abilities, and tasks) required for your job (or one that you aspire to have). Grade yourself on proficiency with each skill (A, B, C, D, or F). Based on your grades, which skills are strengths? Which skills do you need to acquire or enhance to meet the demands of your field?

- Identify learning sources that offer the training or knowledge needed to strengthen competence in the skills for which you have a low grade. Begin by selecting one source (e.g., a book); search resources and find one to consume (e.g., read, watch a video, or take an online course). The key word is "begin!"

13
Abundance or Scarcity?
Mindset Determines Opportunities

Many variables play a role in determining professional success and personal happiness- your skill set, how others perceive you, and the economy, to name but three variables. However, one variable may play a more significant role than any other: Your mindset. The beliefs about yourself and the world around you contained between your ears influence how you react to what happens to you and determines your daily actions.

Mindset is influential in the growth (or stagnation) of your personal brand. Psychologist Carol Dweck has conducted extensive research on mindset. Dweck says people adopt either a fixed mindset or growth mindset. People with a fixed mindset believe their lot in life is determined by the cards they have been dealt-their education level, skills, and relationships. In contrast, people possessing a growth mindset believe their traits and characteristics can be expanded and built upon to pursue new opportunities. A pretty stark contrast- which mindset appeals to you?

The Scarcity Box

A fixed mindset is like relegating one's self to a box, with scarcity being an overarching theme in thoughts and beliefs. People with a fixed mindset have a view that success is a zero-sum game; for some people to enjoy success others will be denied.

Similarly, a fixed mindset leads one to believe that the resources at their disposal are what they are, will not change, and thus their prospects to change and grow are limited. This fear of limited resources can lead to a "lookout for number one" mentality that has the unintended effect of limiting one's growth. When we focus on preserving the resources and relationships we possess, we can miss out on chances to create positive impact on others (and ourselves at the same time).

Be Open to Abundance

In contrast to a fixed mindset view that resources are finite and must be treated as scarce, a growth mindset sees abundance. An abundance mentality holds not only that resources can be added, but they *must* be added and shared with others to add value to people with whom we come in contact. Abundance suggests adding resources is not a win-lose battle; there are plenty of skills, talents, and relationships to go around. It is our duty to ourselves and others to put forth the effort to add to our resources by investing in ourselves through learning, networking, and creating.

A growth mindset inspires helping other people grow. Zig Ziglar said "you can have everything in life you want if you help enough other people get what they want." This quote embodies a growth mindset. It is not just about your own growth. Thinking in terms of abundance frees you to consider how you can benefit other people. A scarcity view makes it difficult, if not impossible to help others because one cannot see beyond protecting resources.

Brand Builder

You can adopt a mindset of scarcity or one of abundance. Only one of them sets the stage for personal and professional growth. Which mindset do you want guiding your life?

- Reflect on the current state of your mindset. Would you characterize it as fixed (scarcity) or growth (abundance)? What core beliefs about yourself and the world around you led to how you characterized your mindset?

- Even people with a growth mindset have limiting beliefs Identify one belief that if you changed would foster more of a growth mindset. State that belief in an affirmative tone. Keep it top-of-mind this week by writing it down and repeating it several times daily.

14

Play to Your Strengths
Leverage What You Do Well to Spur Personal Growth

If you wanted to make a positive impression on someone with a meal but your cooking skills consisted of little more than be able to boil water, you might forgo cooking and instead go to a restaurant. But, if you had the gift of combining ingredients to create tasty dishes, you would likely use your gift and cook a magnificent meal. In each case, you get to the desired end result by knowing your strengths.

Your personal brand growth ultimately depends on you knowing who you are… and who you are not. And of course, knowing who you are is not enough. Playing to your strengths will attract opportunity to you.

What Are Strengths?

It does not take much convincing to make the case that knowing and using strengths can enable us achieve more. The challenge resides in uncovering our strengths. What are you good at doing or being? You may even need to take one step back from that question and ask "what are strengths?"

Executive coach Senia Mayman says strengths are a person's natural inclinations in life. They flow from the values that guide your purpose, which is why reflecting on your purpose must take place early on in personal brand development. Strengths can be found in three areas of your brand Makeup:

- Talent (what your abilities enable)

- Knowledge (what you know)

- Experience (what you have done before).

The good news is that shortcomings in knowledge and experience can be overcome. Thus, using strengths to build and grow your brand comes down to identifying talents.

Uncovering Your Strengths

Knowing strengths are essential to building your aspirational brand is one thing; figuring out your strengths may be a more daunting task. But, it need not be difficult. Find your strengths through the following sources:

- *Reflecting on past successes.* Think of times you experienced personal victories. Chances are one or more strengths (i.e., your natural inclinations) guided you.

- *Ask for feedback from people around you (parents, co-workers, friends, or teachers).* While not everyone will give the candid feedback you need, getting input from people who observe your strengths regularly are in a unique position to help. Others may see talents on display that you do not realize create value.

- *Build relationship with a mentor vested in your development.* Leadership expert and author Micheal Burt says "everyone needs a coach in life." One way having a mentor benefits you is he or she can offer an objective evaluation of your talents and give counsel how to use them to your advantage.

Strengths can work for you, but you have to put them to work. Own your brand development by identifying so that you can leverage strengths to your advantage. They will do you little good if you sit back and wait for opportunities to put strengths to work to land on your doorstep.

Brand Builder

Finding a fit between personal strengths, passion, and market need is the sweet spot where you can be rewarded for creating value for others while doing work you love. Gain clarity on your strengths by:

- Compile an inventory of your talents, knowledge, and experience. Begin by doing a self-assessment, but also get input from others who know you well. Feedback from others is a must because you may possess strengths that you downplay or don't even recognize. Or, you may be over-valuing some traits in which you are not as strong as you believe.

- Complement your information gathering efforts with objective feedback in the form of personal strengths assessments. Two widely used assessments are the Gallup StrengthsFinder and the Values in Action survey of character strengths. Take one (or both) of these assessments to give you another layer of information about your strengths.

15
Thrive on Weaknesses
Dealing with Limitations Imposed by Weaknesses

Some people believe spending time and energy on identifying and trying to overcome weaknesses is an exercise in futility. Instead, they advocate focusing on strengths that can serve you well (the theme of "Play to Your Strengths"). Ignoring weaknesses or otherwise pretending they do not exist is not beneficial to brand development. Why? Doing so means you miss out on opportunities to recognize thoughts or behaviors that could be limiting your performance and growth.

Instead of allowing weaknesses to be a liability to your brand, thrive on weaknesses by committing to three steps.

Admit It

Recognizing that you have weaknesses is not a weakness in itself. Face it, you are not going to be great at everything. Admitting weaknesses can be a positive move for your brand as it reveals authenticity. You're not expected to be perfect- any brand that suggests perfection is lying.

Admitting weaknesses frees you to determine what they are. One approach to uncovering weaknesses is to seek input from others (family, friend, or mentor) to pinpoint traits or behaviors that could be working to your brand's detriment. This feedback will enable you to detect your own "blind spot" and take steps toward improvement.

Another approach to recognizing weaknesses that you can undertake yourself is employing the process of reverse engineering. Identify the hard and soft skills most important to the job you want. Then, acknowledge whether you have weaknesses among those key skills.

Detail It

Admitting weakness is a crucial first step. From there, specify how the weakness is limiting pursuit of your goals or personal growth. Have you been passed over for a job or promotion because of the weakness? Does it have a negative effect on your self-image? Understanding *how* the weakness is limiting brand potential can be powerful motivation to address it.

Set quantifiable goals with the aim of overcoming the weakness. If you admit that shyness limits your effectiveness at networking events, set a goal of attending one networking event a month during the next year. And, for each networking event you attend, set a goal of meeting three people at the event and follow up with an email or LinkedIn connection request. You can't improve what you can't measure, so be sure that you detail actions to be taken to deal with weaknesses that are a drag on your personal brand.

Go For It

The first two steps are necessary, but not sufficient conditions for thriving on weaknesses. The final step is to take action. Sales expert and motivational speaker Brian Tracy refers to "eating the frog" when talking about doing something that you would prefer to postpone or do not look forward to doing. Eat the frog right away; don't dwell on it or think about it. Then, it is done.

Similarly, take your weaknesses head on, whether it is reluctance to engage in networking, dealing with conflict, lack of empathy, or whatever limiting attributes you identify and work to address. It is not necessary to transform weaknesses into strengths, but refusal to apply the three steps of managing weaknesses is a choice to not give your brand a chance to realize its full potential.

Brand Builder

Possessing weaknesses is normal. How you choose to approach weaknesses can be the difference between removing weaknesses as barriers to growth and having a personal brand that does not meet its potential. Employ the three-step process for managing weaknesses:

- *Admit your weaknesses.* Whether you ask for input from people who know you or conduct self-assessment (or use both approaches), recognize your weaknesses.

- *Detail the impact of your weaknesses.* Recognizing weaknesses may not be enough to prompt you to act on overcoming them, but reflecting on the harm or limitations weaknesses impose on your brand might make you uncomfortable to the point of be willing to do something about them. Set quantifiable goals for improvement.

- *Go for it.* Plans start you down the path to overcoming weaknesses, but ultimately you must take the necessary actions to carry out your plan and meet improvement goals.

16
Stay in Your Lane
The Importance of Brand Positioning

A characteristic of a brand that is often misunderstood is who owns a brand. While the person or organization owns rights to a brand name and brand marks like a logo, a brand's value resides in the thoughts and beliefs held about it in the minds of customers and others. You do not own your brand as much as you work to influence how people perceive it.

The fact that we cede control of our brands can be a frightening thought, but one strategy rescues us from becoming lost in a sea of sameness: Positioning. A brand's position is its standing in the minds of an audience relative to other brands. In other words, what is different or unique about your brand that sets you apart?

The basis of brand positioning is *one thing* about your brand that is a differentiator. People cannot remember everything about you, so what is the one trait or fact that should instantly be associated with you in which you stand out from the pack? Any personal branding tactics used should relate to your brand position. Think of it as staying in your lane- you get to pick the lane in which you will drive, but you get to the desired destination by staying in your lane rather than weaving in and out of lanes.

When picking your lane that is your brand's positioning, check your point of difference against two criteria: 1) is it real and 2) is it relevant?

Be Real

We live in a world filled with self-proclaimed experts, gurus, and thought leaders. These points of difference are shallow claims or outright exaggerations if not backed up with a strong makeup of strengths (i.e., combination of hard and soft skills). Your point of difference has to actually exist- you must possess it. When a business makes claims about a product and cannot deliver, customer trust can erode. Similarly, if you do not live up to your brand position you could lose the trust of the very people you seek to influence.

If you pick a lane for your brand position in which you do not belong you will stand out among the other drivers... but for the wrong reasons. Look to your brand makeup- hard skills learned, soft skills developed, and personal strengths possessed- to find your point of difference.

Be Relevant

Having a real point of difference is important in creating a distinctive brand position, but its effectiveness depends on relevance to others. Does your point of difference enable you to add value to the people you serve? How do people benefit from your brand's point of difference? Relevance is crucial given that brands are made up of perceptions that reside in the minds of the marketplace.

How do you determine what makes a brand position relevant? It requires understanding the audience you serve. What are their needs? Are there certain "pain points" they have that you can soothe through the value you offer? You might possess a real point of difference, but if it holds little importance to your audience it is not a meaningful basis for brand position.

Brand Builder

Establishing a brand position and delivering on it consistently can have significant impact on differentiating your personal brand. The decision is not if you need a brand position but what it should be. Make that decision by doing the following:

- Determine a real point of difference that you possess, is noticed by others, and is one of your strengths. You can identify it on your own, or consult a friend or mentor who knows your abilities and strengths. You do not have to be best-in-world at whatever your differentiating characteristic is; you only need to be able to communicate that you are different or unique compared to others in the same job or field.

- Is the point of difference you identified relevant to others? Will it provide benefit or value to them? Or, is it little more than an interesting fact about you? If it adds value to the point that your differentiator could be the reason why you are hired, promoted, or able to influence other people, it could be used to position your brand.

17
Your Story is Your Brand
Storytelling Defines You

Take a moment to think of someone who has made an impression upon you. Whether that person is someone you have known for a long time or you only had one encounter, chances are you were impacted by a story the person told. A story can be entertaining, captivating, informing, and the same story can touch people in different ways.

One of the most poignant stories that I recall is the college experience of my friend, Colby. I have heard Colby share a story about his first year in college. He recounts how he struggled to make the transition to college as well as the football team that had brought him to that college. Colby says he called his parents and told them he wanted to come home. Their response was straightforward- "no." His parents knew quitting and coming home was the easy way out.

Most of the young people who hear his story learn the importance on not giving up on something that you want badly. I took away a different message, and that is that my friend had to overcome adversity to get through that rough period. He is successful today, but he took his lumps along the way, strengthening him in the process.

Colby's story is noteworthy because he is a person who attracts others to him. One reason he connects with friends and strangers alike is that they relate to him through the stories that define his personal brand. You, too have stories that have shaped who you are and how you will take on the future. However, those stories will not benefit your brand unless they are revealed.

Why Stories Matter

Telling a story is an effective communication technique. Stories are impactful because:

- *They are memorable.* Stories often contain emotional elements that let us empathize with the storyteller.

- *They stand out from other messages.* I first heard Colby's college story several years ago, and it rises above virtually all of the other interactions I have had with him since then.

- *They connect people ("I can relate to you").* I have observed Colby telling his first-year college story several times, and each time I notice that the audience of college students sees someone like them in his story of self-doubt.

- *Builds trust ("you are similar to me").* Revealing your story can remove uncertainty about your intentions and motivations, particularly with people who do not know you well.

An important point to note about stories is although a story may be told in the context of something that happened to or involved you, the focal point of the story must be the receiver of the message. Your story does more than sell you. It enlightens others as to how they can benefit from the message in your story.

You Have a Story

On the first day I meet students at the beginning of a semester, they supply information about themselves to me so that I can get to know them. One bit of information I sometimes request is that they complete the statement "an interesting fact about me is…" Occasionally, a student's response is "nothing—

there is nothing about me that is interesting." That answer exhibits tremendous modesty at the very least. You *do* have interesting facts about yourself that comprise your personal brand story. But, you must resist any thoughts of hiding those stories from the world. Instead, embrace your stories as defining moments in building your brand.

Many approaches can be found for bringing your stories to life. A good starting point is for you to answer the following questions about yourself:

- *What path did you take to get to where you are?* Think of Colby's first-year college story as an example of a path-charting story.

- *What or who inspired you?* As stated in the chapter introduction, we all have people in our lives whose story influence our own story.

- *What values define you?* Themes of your story often relate to brand Meaning, your foundational purpose, values, and passion.

- *How can you set yourself apart and succeed in your industry?* Stories serve to make you more interesting in the minds of others. You may be similar to others who do the same thing, but your story can differentiate you from the pack.

Once you are equipped with answers to these questions you begin to craft your story in a way that is not only interesting to others, but your story also has value for others because it helps them in some way (e.g., solve a problem or spark an idea).

Brand Builder

Telling stories that are the story of your brand is not an optional endeavor—you must incorporate storytelling into efforts

71

to manage your professional identity. Before telling your story, take the following steps:

- Identify a person (or persons) who has touched you through stories. What story traits resonate with you? What can you take away from how these stories are told that you would feel comfortable adapting to telling your own story?

- Determine who is the audience for your story (i.e., who will it matter to?). Is it customers? Employees? Investors? Peers? State the needs and wants of your audience and how your story can help move them toward meeting needs or wants in some way. In other words, your audience is asking "what's in it for me?" when listening to your story. What is the answer to that question?

18
Weave a Support Net
The Importance of Networking

Have you ever heard someone utter any of the following statements?

- *It's not what you know but who you know that determines if you get ahead.*

- *It's not who you know, it's who knows you.*

- *Alone we can do so little; together we can do so much.*

The message taken from these statements is that it is rare for accomplishment, growth, and ultimately, success to be realized on your own. Even the most self-sufficient personality types will find the horizon of opportunity limited if they think it is unimportant to invest in building a network of contacts.

In other words, networking is not an option! Get over it—you have to do it. Better yet, when you realize the benefits of networking you will wonder why anyone would believe they can get along just fine without building a network.

What Networking Is... and Isn't

Trying to wrap your arms around the concept of networking and how to do contributes to the reluctance and outright fear many people have about networking. What does it mean to network? Why is it so important? Those questions are legitimate. Simplifying the concept can put you at ease and clarify what to do in order to build a valuable professional network.

My favorite definition of networking is simple:

Building better relationships.

73

No seven-step process to complete, no sophisticated training required; just a focus on building better relationships with the people in your life.

Equating networking with building better relationships also indicates the frequency with which you should be concerned with networking: Always. Like building your personal brand in general, there is no stop or end date once you begin. Why would you want to stop if the practice of networking leads to building better relationships?

The definition "building better relationships" tells you what networking is. It is also useful to recognize what networking is not. Networking can be equated with being some kind of contest, one in which a person tries to get as many business cards as possible at an event or a large number of connections on LinkedIn. Networking is not pursuing notches on a belt. Quality relationships trumps quantity of connections every time.

And, if you think networking will help you get what you want, forget it. Networking can help you get what you want… if you are committed to helping other people get what *they* want. To "get" from networking, you must first give- time, attention, assistance, advice- be helpful to others so that they want to reciprocate and return that value to you when needed.

A Networking Green Thumb

In order to reap the benefits of networking, you must commit to the act of networking when you do *not* need it. Just as a gardener enjoys a bountiful yield by planting seeds, nurturing them with fertilizer, water, and continuous care, your success in building a professional network hinges on growth rather than harvesting. Will you tap your network for assistance- a favor, introduction, or recommendation? Absolutely, you will. However, that is not the purpose of developing your network.

Are you willing to do the following?

- Commit a block of time daily to networking with social media connections (and make new connections)

- Make yourself available to meet new people when attending meetings or events

- Connect people you know to others who might benefit from your introduction

- Be a cheerleader or supporter for people in your network as they achieve success (e.g., earn a promotion or receive an award).

A common thread running through these actions is they build better relationships, our working definition of networking.

Brand Builder

Growing a professional network requires persistence and a commitment to building better relationships. Strengthen your networking efforts through the following steps:

- On a scale of 1 to 10, with 1 being "very uncomfortable" and 10 being "very comfortable," rate your comfort level with face-to-face networking. In addition to the numeric rating, reflect on why you gave yourself that score. If your rating was 7 or less, identify limitations or personal weaknesses holding you back from being more comfortable as a networker. If you rated yourself 8 or higher, identify traits or strengths you possess that would enable you to grow your network.

- Create a plan in which you spend at least 30 minutes a day, five days a week, engaged in networking activities on social media. Be specific how you will spend the time such as reading and commenting on blogs, sharing or commenting on LinkedIn updates from people in your network.

- Set a weekly networking goal (e.g., adding five new connections a week on LinkedIn; requesting introductions to three different people). Keep in mind that the goal set should go beyond merely adding to the total connections in your network- have a strategy for the growth that you want to realize.

19
Share That You Care
Leverage the Law of Reciprocity

Leadership expert John Maxwell said "people don't care how much you know until they know how much you care." This statement has huge implications for your personal brand. If you want to build a distinctive brand, it should not be done on knowledge or skill alone. Do those qualities matter? Absolutely yes! However, a dazzling display of what you know will likely not build trust among people to the point that they will take action when prompted by you. They need to know how much you care, and practicing "share that you care" can go a long way toward building trust and instilling confidence in others.

It's about Reciprocity

A payoff of personal branding is creating influence that is exerted to persuade others. Your objective may be to elicit a response (e.g., sign up for an email list) or make a commitment such as agreeing to do business with you. How do you arrive at having that level of influence?

The heart of influence is reciprocity, the inclination of someone to want to give back to you. Community membership (e.g., among your peers, in your company, with your customers, or with classmates) is a powerful motivator for reciprocity and ultimately, influence.

A tenet of reciprocity is in order to be recognized as a valuable individual you must first be viewed as a *trusted* community member. The return on investment from reciprocity is what you give to a community, you earn in return. Notice that what is secondary is what *you* get from being part of a community. You get when you give, and not before. And, you do not give because you expect to get... but you will likely receive value because you have given of yourself to the community. Influence is realized when you become a valued part of a community.

Engaging = Caring

John Maxwell's quote on showing that you care appropriately emphasizes being of value to others as a means of demonstrating your own brand value. You may be sold on the concept but are unsure how to put it into action. How do you show that you care? You do it by initiating communication and interaction. In short: *engage*. A definition of engage is to "occupy, attract, or involve (someone's interest or attention)." Engagement starts with you being willing to comment, share, or like. It is no different than starting a conversation; someone has to start.

Engaging is the first step toward creating brand value and ultimately, influence. Social networking sites make sharing easier than ever- like, comment, share, or forward- can be done in mere clicks. Initiating interaction while acknowledging the value of others is very effective for planting the seeds of reciprocity. But, engagement is not limited to digital channels. Don't overlook face-to-face opportunities that enable you to actively take an interest in others by making introductions, asking questions, and starting conversations.

Brand Builder

Sharing is a valuable practice for establishing your value to a community. Embrace "share that you care" by doing the following during the next week:

- Set aside 15 minutes of each day you spend time on social media to focus on demonstrating caring. Comment on a blog post or other content posted by someone in your community, share or like content you find interesting or valuable, or initiate conversation with someone by giving a compliment or asking a question. Building sharing time into your social media activity will establish sharing as a practice.

- Identify three people that you would like to influence in some way. Reflect on how you could use sharing tactics to be communicate your value to these people.

20
Steal Like An Artist
Complement Originality with Imitation

It is not unusual for personal branding advocates to exhort us to "be authentic" and "find your voice." This advice is well intentioned, but it could lead to feelings of inadequacy about the originality of our brand. Do not take these suggestions as a requirement that you make only new-to-the-world contributions. If that were the case, we would all be in trouble!

Most innovation today comes from improvements or new twists on existing ideas, concepts, or products. If you think of innovation as "creating new value," you free yourself from the pressure to create something original to feel you have contributions to make. And to innovate, you can and should build on what is already known and exists. Artist and author Austin Kleon dubbed this idea "steal like an artist" in his book of the same title.

Learning by Imitating

If you want to bring new value to the table, you must first become a value creator. Chances are you are not born that way; you acquire knowledge, skills, and abilities that put you in a position to be an innovator. Imitating other people and behaviors can be the starting point for learning that enables you to deliver new value:

Copying → Understanding → Modifying → Learning

Learning is a natural process we employ regularly using these four steps.

Be Free to Copy

Don't feel inadequate or that you have taken a shortcut because you learned through imitation. Originality is more myth than reality; nearly all innovation arises from imitating what we observe. Psychologist Lev Vygotsky observed "through others we become ourselves." Not only is copying acceptable, but you should seek out opportunities to become yourself through others.

Of course, there is a difference between imitation and plagiarism. When one plagiarizes, he or she attempts to pass off work as their own rather than giving credit to its creator. Imitation is the result of gathering and interpreting other works, being influenced by the value you see in it.

Think about an accomplished music artist- that person or group usually points to one or more other artists that shaped the sound of their music. Are they copycats of their influences? Almost always, the answer is "no." Perhaps you can hear similarities with artists that influenced them, but they are not direct knockoffs.

You, too, should embrace the freedom that comes from not having to be original. Who can you look to for inspiration or as an example? Multiple influences are not only acceptable, but they are expected. You can draw from others to help shape your brand Meaning, Makeup, and Message. Chances are influencers will impact one of those areas but not necessarily two or all three of them.

Brand Builder

We are wired to learn by copying. Allow yourself to be open to influences from people and works you find valuable. Steal like an artist this week by:

- Identify someone who you see as having influence with you (i.e., you like, admire, or share beliefs). Reflect on the characteristics of that person that draw you to him or her. What can you learn from that characteristic of the person that would be beneficial to your personal brand?

- Reach out to someone who you have not met previously that you feel has influenced you. Send the person an email, tweet, direct message, or through face-to-face communication. Let him or her know how you have been influenced. If the person responds, you may have made a valuable addition to your network. If not, at least you have expressed gratitude for the influence and acknowledged growth by imitation.

21
Listen Up
Learning by Listening

Whether you realize it or not, listening is hard work. Good listening skills are essential for being an effective communicator, yet its importance does not seem to be recognized. It is common to see job announcements seek candidates with strong oral and written communication skills. Can you recall seeing an employer list "good listener" as a desired trait in describing the ideal candidate? Is the general lack of mention mean listening is unimportant?

Of course listening is important, but again, it is hard work. And, most of us aren't very good at it. Research from the 1950s by Ralph Nichols and Leonard Stevens found that people retained only about half of the information to that they heard. That retention rate was what they remembered immediately after message exposure. Information retention rate six months later dropped to about 25 percent. The conclusion to be reached by Nichols' and Stevens' research was apparent: Most people do not know how to listen. Oh sure, we have ears that enable us to hear. But, we lack the skills to use our ears effectively for communication.

I cannot help but wonder what the results would be if Nichols and Stevens conducted their study today. Our attention span is stretched by text messages, push notifications, and social network feeds. How can we deal with these distractions and get the most out of listening to others? Practice the two Ms of listening: mindset and methodology.

The Listening Mindset

The first step toward becoming an effective listener is making the conscious decision to listen. Sounds strange perhaps, but hearing words from another person does not equal listening. You must set the stage for listening (and greater message retention). The listening mindset can be achieved by doing the following:

- *Show empathy.* You must care about what the other person is saying.

- *Have an open mind.* In other words, check your assumptions. You cannot process the information someone gives you if you are busy passing judgment on what you are hearing.

- *Be attentive.* Listening is a choice. You can choose to focus your attention and mind on the other person, or you can choose to sneak peeks at your phone.

- *Be relaxed.* Allow yourself the freedom to listen. If you are thinking about what you have to do later in the day or this weekend's party you are not listening in the moment.

- *Try to feel what speaker is feeling.* Listening and observing the speaker's emotions can add an additional layer of meaning to the words you hear. Look to make connections between the speaker's words and emotional state.

- *Have curiosity.* Recognize that listening is a learning opportunity. Ask open-ended questions to draw deeper understanding (also shows empathy and interest).

You can learn every tried-and-true listening technique, but if you do not allow yourself to be in the proper frame of mind to listen they will not work.

The Listening Methodology

If you are in search of tips and techniques to become a better listener, you're in luck. The methodology of listening has no shortage of tools at your disposal. Keep in mind that these tools will have limited effectiveness if a listening mindset is not adopted:

- *Make eye contact with other person.* Looking at the person with whom you are speaking shows you are listening and care about what the person has to say. Those two messages are significant in today's multi-task, multi-screen world.

- *Picture what person is saying.* The brain is a powerful visual production machine. Go beyond processing words to create imagery of what you hear.

- *Don't interrupt.* Making eye contact and creating visual imagery of what the other person is saying goes a long way toward minimizing you becoming a disruption to the communication process. In short- zip it and listen!

- *Ask questions only for understanding.* Questions can demonstrate empathy and lead to richer communication. Questions asked should be to aid understanding; be careful not to ask questions that take conversation to a different topic.

- *Don't impose your own solutions.* You do not have to offer an answer to every situation. Offer your viewpoint if asked but do not feel it is required.

- *Pay attention to nonverbal cues.* Learn from what is not being said; does the speaker's body posture, facial expressions, or hand gestures that convey additional meaning?

- *Embrace silence.* It seems counterintuitive that silence is equated with effective communication. But, sometimes a pregnant pause allows you to process information and reflect on a message.

You may look at the above list of listening techniques and reach the conclusion that effective listening is rooted in common courtesy and common sense. You would be correct to make that determination. Unfortunately, too many people do not show either or both when communicating with others. The result is missed opportunities to learn and in turn, to potentially be of greater value to others.

Brand Builder

If your listening skills do not need to be strengthened, you may skip these brand builders and read on. Still here? I thought so! Use listening as a means of learning and enhancing your value by focusing on the following:

- Identify one of the seven tactics in The Listening Methodology section that if improved upon would make you a better listener. For example, if you recognize that you often interrupt people during conversations, commit to minimizing interruptions. What action must you take to implement the tactic?

22
Networking is not Fatal
Overcome Fears to Build Better Relationships

Does the word "networking" trigger a reaction akin to rubbing poison ivy leaves on your arms? For many people, the thought of engaging in networking is unappealing and even unsettling. Even established, experienced professionals can have feelings like "What could I possibly have to offer?" "What am I supposed to say?" or "No one at a networking event would want to talk with me." If you have had feelings like this about networking, turns out you're normal... even if your feelings are misguided.

Unless you are a seasoned networker, you have work to do to become more effective at building relationships with others. But, do not be intimidated by this challenge. It can be reduced to two steps: 1) Recognizing networking fears and 2) overcoming those fears.

Recognize Networking Fears

The existence of networking fears is not a matter of if they exist, only the degree to which fear impedes your ability to network effectively. In extreme cases, fear keeps people hanging out more in the restroom than the meeting area or worse, on their living room sofa. Many fears can be cited as obstacles to networking, but most of them can be classified as one of three worries:

- *I won't be liked.* Striking up a conversation with strangers can be daunting. Ever walk into a room and seemingly everyone is engrossed in conversation? Everyone except you, that is. Can I make a good first impression that will move people to like me, not shun me?

- *I won't be valued.* Even if I get past the mental barrier of feeling accepted, will I have anything to offer that makes others appreciate my value? Of you course you do, but that barrier makes it difficult for you to see.

- *I won't be accepted.* You may feel that people can tolerate you in a brief interaction, but a brief encounter does not equal getting buy-in from others. But, if you focus on how you can create value for others you go a long way toward gaining acceptance. Why? You have made interactions with others about them, not you.

Networking fears can be intensified for introverts. Concerns about being liked, valued, and accepted are magnified for those of us who find it difficult to build rapport with people we do not know. This is not to say that introverts are given a pass when it comes to networking. On the contrary, we must work harder to understand our networking fears and realize we are not much different than everyone else about feelings toward networking.

Overcome Networking Fears

Understanding that networking fears are normal and likely held by the very people you are nervous about interacting with is an initial step toward becoming more comfortable with networking. The outlook you take toward networking can minimize apprehension and transform networking from a chore to a strength of your brand. Become proactive about networking by putting the following steps in action:

- *Have a plan.* Don't just show up at a networking event. Do research on who will be there. Another aspect of planning is having an objective in terms of number of new people to meet or specific attendees you want to meet.

- *Make a good first impression.* Put yourself in other people's shoes— if you were them would you want to spend time in conversation with you? Smile, make eye contact, and take a genuine interest in others. Otherwise, you may unwittingly send a message of being closed off from conversations.

- *Listen.* Your value to others is heavily dependent upon knowing their story, dreams, and needs. You will know none of that unless you commit to listening to them. Focus on the other person (not what you plan to say next) in order to understand them and how you might be of value.

- *Step out of your comfort zone.* You may feel that networking requires you step out of your comfort zone. Even if you are not terrified at the prospect of engaging strangers in conversation, you must make yourself open to growth by not limiting yourself to spending time with people you know already.

Change your outlook on networking to focus on the benefits. Networking is an efficient means of meeting new business prospects. Also, there is a social aspect in that you can meet new people.

Brand Builder

Rather than letting networking fears hold you back from meeting new people and contributing to your personal growth, consider the potential of networking to be a brand strength.

Implement the two steps of understanding networking fears and overcoming them by doing the following:

- Engage in candid self-reflection about your attitude toward networking. If you have fears about networking, what are they? How do these fears limit effectiveness of your networking efforts?

- Think about someone you know who is an effective networker. What traits or practices contribute to his or her networking success? If you selected one trait or practice that person employs and adopted as your own to improve your own networking, which one would it be? Why?

23
(RSS) Feed Yourself
Create a Go-To List of Blogs

Imagine a world in which the latest ideas and information from a field of interest were available at a click of your web browser. You had access to authoritative sources and eccentric minds alike. No need to imagine such a world—it exists already. Reading for self-improvement has never been more convenient or affordable. Rather than being limited to consuming information curated for you by a newspaper or magazine, you are chief editor of your reading regimen.

The vast content available on the web can be intimidating. How do you sort through the plethora of websites and blogs to pinpoint only those sources that offer relevant content for you? RSS feed readers.

It's Really Simple

Perhaps you have heard of RSS or RSS feeders but were unsure what it meant. The most common usage of RSS is as an acronym for Really Simple Syndication. As an information consumer, using RSS enables you to receive new content from a website as it is published. Rather than checking your favorite blog to see if a new post has been published, an RSS feed reader will deliver content to you when available. An RSS reader has an advantage over email newsletters to which you subscribe in that you do not have to give your email address or other personal information to receive content.

Another way that an RSS reader lives up to the "simple" in RSS is ease of access and use. Among your choices for pulling together RSS feeds into a single location online are Feedly, My Yahoo, My MSN, and Flipboard. Each of these RSS readers offers a slightly different user experience, so try them all to find a format you like.

RSS Strengthens Your Brand

You may look at RSS more as a convenience to gather interesting content than as a tool to build your personal brand. However, customizing a learning program using RSS can enhance the Makeup and Message dimensions of your brand. And you thought it was just a shortcut to finding interesting information! RSS can aid in brand development by:

- Introducing you to new concepts, practices, or trends, adding to your knowledge (part of Makeup).

- Exposing you to diverse viewpoints, including ones that are different from your own. Expanding diversity of thought can strengthen critical thinking skills (part of Makeup).

- Reading blogs that invite comments set the stage for networking opportunities when you interact with the author and other readers (part of Message).

Not many aspects of building and manage a brand can be characterized as really simple, but bringing order and structure to self-study using an RSS reader is an exception.

Brand Builder

Whether you are using an RSS reader already or just now discovering it, enjoy the benefits of RSS by doing the following:

- Compile a list of websites and blogs whose content relates to your interests (if you already use an RSS reader, review RSS feeds you receive and consider adding new ones and removing ones you read rarely). Use one of the RSS readers mentioned (Feedly, My Yahoo, My MSN, or Flipboard) to deliver new content from interesting websites or blogs. Set aside a certain time each day (e.g., while you have your morning coffee or during lunch break) to open your RSS reader and check out new content available.

- If you subscribe to a blog's RSS feed, take advantage of networking opportunities by leaving a comment for the blog author or responding to another reader's comments. Remember that RSS feeds not only have the potential to enlighten you; they can expand your network, too.

24
The Missing Link
Why You Need a LinkedIn Presence

You may have heard LinkedIn referred to as "Facebook for business." It is like Facebook in that it is a social networking website that lets you connect with friends and strangers alike. The similarities may end there as LinkedIn is geared toward amplifying your personal brand, making business connections, and even landing a job.

LinkedIn actually had a head start on most of its social media counterparts, launching in 2003 ahead of massive networks like Facebook, Twitter, and Instagram. Today, LinkedIn has more than 430 million users worldwide, including nearly 130 million users in the United States. LinkedIn's users are rather active as the site has 106 million unique visitors monthly.

These stats may prove little to you other than LinkedIn attracts a lot of interest and traffic. Those qualities might not help your brand... or will they?

The Value Proposition

LinkedIn is a valuable personal branding resource regardless of your career stage. Whether you are starting out and looking for an entry level opportunity or are an established professional, LinkedIn can make you more visible, lead you to new people, and influence how others perceive you. Specifically, LinkedIn's benefits include:

- *Build a network of contacts that you might need later.* Networking experts call this practice "digging a well before you're thirsty".

- *Recruiters look for candidates to fill jobs.* Many open positions are filled by people who were not looking for jobs. Recruiters were attracted to their personal brands via their LinkedIn profile.

- *Industry groups can keep you informed.* The Groups feature is one of LinkedIn's greatest sources of value. Group interactions can keep you up to date on news and trends as well as add to people in your field that you know.

- *Prompts use to keep résumé information up to date.* Your LinkedIn profile is like your personal marketing brochure, minus printing costs! You can easily update and add new content to your profile.

- *Influence what people think about you via content you post.* What you share and post tells people a great deal about who you are, what you believe, and what you know.

- *Showcase your accomplishments and skills.* Don't worry that you are going overboard on self-promotion. Your profile, status updates, and other content posted is intended in part to market yourself. If you don't do it, who will?

These six items are not a comprehensive list of how LinkedIn can help your brand, but they represent some of the most compelling reasons to commit to using LinkedIn to build your brand.

Avoiding LinkedIn

Not everyone is sold on the branding payoffs of LinkedIn. Like most situations when we do not adopt a product, the underlying reason is lack of understanding about how the product satisfies needs or wants. Rather than risk venturing into the unknown or investing time to learn, we maintain status quo.

More people with whom I talk about LinkedIn indicate they at least have an account. But, I still run into many people who resist setting up a LinkedIn account. The reasons? These responses are among the most common:

- *I have a job already.* Congratulations, but remember that line about digging a well before you're thirsty? I can often tell when someone has just lost his job. He gets active on LinkedIn suddenly. The problem is networking is an ongoing activity, not one that matters only when looking for a job.

- *My boss might think I'm looking for a job if she sees me using LinkedIn.* This reason has more validity. I have heard employers say they do not want their employees using social media on the job because they may be using the time to look for another job. However, if your role involves interacting with people from other companies it would benefit your employer (and probably your paycheck) to network on LinkedIn.

- *I don't do social media.* It's hard to be on LinkedIn if you have an aversion to social media in general. Passing on LinkedIn is your prerogative; so is my decision to pass on you as a potential employee because I lack awareness or knowledge of you.

For many recruiters, the search engine has replaced the résumé as the go to information source. One survey found that 94% of hiring managers check out a prospective employee's online footprint, including LinkedIn. If you have no presence or a weak network, decision makers are left to make judgments about the strength of your professional network. Leave no doubt about your ability to make connections and offer value to others-be on LinkedIn!

Brand Builder

You can market yourself to the entire world by establishing a presence on LinkedIn. If you do not have a LinkedIn account, sign up for one. If you have a LinkedIn account but not happy with its content, this exercise is for you, too. Work on creating a LinkedIn presence by doing the following:

- Connect with people you already know- family, co-workers friends- the low hanging fruit that your real life connections are. You will be surprised who your connections know that you do not (but would like to know).

- Remember LinkedIn is like face-to-face networking in that you have to be interested to be interesting. Show you are listening to others by liking, commenting, or sharing content from at least one of your connections daily. You will find as you give love and approval, you are likely to get the same in return.

25
Go on a Diet
Manage Intake of Information "Calories"

A spreading illness threatens the productivity and well-being of millions of people around the world. Sadly, there is no known vaccine or prescription drug available to treat this condition. Symptoms include distraction, ignoring people around you, and fear of missing out (or FOMO for short).

You may have guessed by now that this illness is internet addiction. Describing excessive amounts of time spent online as an addiction is not an over-the-top attempt to get attention. Some mental health professionals see internet addiction as the next mental illness.

One challenge arising from treating addiction is arriving at an objective measure of what is excessive amount of time spent online. If you spend 30 hours a week online doing research as part of your job, is your situation different from the person who spends 30 hours a week online playing World of Warcraft? Is time spent chatting with family members online viewed differently than time spent chatting with strangers?

What is or is not internet addiction will be left to the appropriate experts. The point is time spent online could be a threat to your personal brand, regardless of what you are doing. Ironically, this effect could be occurring as you engage in activities you believe are beneficial to brand development).

Nothing New

Spending too much time online is the latest diversion we have found to give us enjoyment… or refuge from tasks we should be doing. In addition to spending time on the internet, people manage to procrastinate by:

- Reading

- Talking (in-person or on the phone)

- Watching TV

- Engaging in exercise or other leisure activities

- Playing video games.

The difference between these activities and being tethered to our smartphones is how always being connected to the internet magnifies the distractions we face. Americans check their social media accounts an average of 17 times a day. That figure rises to about 40 times a day in Argentina, Malaysia, and Mexico. Simply put, time spent engaging in this activity takes us away from other uses of time that could aid our development.

Dietary Guidelines

A solution to managing the enormous volume of news and entertainment content at our fingertips is the concept of a diet. Connotations with diet often are restrictive notions of what you cannot eat. But, an information diet (like any diet) should focus on making positive, healthy choices that increase the odds of achieving desired outcomes.

Two essential pieces in your information diet include:

- *Recognize the threats.* Just as we can be tipped off to the need for a food diet by tight-fitting pants, look for signs that time spent online is hindering your productivity or growth. One of the most common reasons people spend inordinate amounts of time online is they are procrastinating, avoiding something else they should be doing. In his book *Take the Stairs*, speaker and consultant Rory Vaden acknowledges procrastination is often an intentional effort to delay doing something that we should be doing.

In other cases, procrastination occurs in the name of "busy." We are checking email, interacting with others on social media, and chatting with co-workers. Although we want to justify these tasks as work or necessary time investments, the reality is often we are not using time wisely.

- *Manage the threats.* Admitting to squandering time or working online without a plan is an important first step toward better time management. The other step required is committing to take actions that manage how you spend time online. You may have heard the saying "you can't manage what you can't measure." Manage your time online by tracking it. One approach is to schedule time for social media or email and get off when time is up. A Pomodoro timer, available on web sites or in app form, is a popular method for setting boundaries on work time and can be applied to tasks you complete using the internet. A common rhythm associated with a Pomodoro timer is 25-minute work periods followed by a short five-minute break.

  Another approach to managing time is to use web sites or apps that do just that- track the amount of time spent online. Not only can these tools tell you how much time you spend online and where time is being spent, some of them can even block you from visiting certain web sites while you are online if your self-control needs an assist.

Brand Builder

The purpose of this reflection is not to pass judgment on how you spend time. Rather, it is an acknowledgement that how we manage time will have significant impact on how much we accomplish compared to our potential as well as relative to competition. That said, binge watching dramas on Netflix will not move you closer to excelling in your field! Set the stage for aligning thoughts and actions toward time management:

- Identify an opportunity for improvement in making better use of your time by pinpointing an online behavior that would benefit from being modified (e.g., checking Facebook fewer times a day or spending less time in email). Set a specific goal for managing time online this week for this improvement opportunity.

26
Recharge Batteries
Personal Renewal Boosts Productivity

It is easy to fall into a trap of working long hours in the name of getting things done, particularly early on in a career or venture. However, one of the secrets to productivity that often does not become apparent until later on is the importance of rest and relaxation. Taking time off refreshes the body and reinvigorates the mind. Unfortunately, learning this valuable secret occurs only after too many long work days, dealing with stressful events and people, and diminished joy coming from the work we do.

The tendency to plow ourselves into our work at the expense of personal well-being is impacted by internal and external forces. We are driven internally to grow and advance. We may convince ourselves the process can be accelerated if we stay at the office an extra hour, make ourselves available to answer email at virtually any moment, or steal a few minutes at night or on the weekend to tick off an item on our To Do list.

Externally, we may fall into the trap of comparing ourselves to others in terms of hours spent working. Or, we are worried what co-workers and bosses think about time we spend on the job. It's not a contest to see who can spend the most hours in the office or reply to emails in the shortest time, but our competitive nature and desire for approval can make us susceptible to treating hours worked as a badge of honor.

Give Me a Break

If you think the amount of time you work crimps effectiveness, you are not alone. Research conducted by The Energy

Project found that 74% of employees have a "personal energy crisis." Deadlines, constant connectivity, and fear of missing out place a strain on workers. Work-life imbalance is a problem for American workers in particular. According to *Harvard Business Review*, 1 out of 4 Americans do not receive paid vacation from their employer. And, more than half of workers who do get paid time off expect to end up working some during their break.

The need to take time off is more significant than being a nice employee perk- your body needs a break. Think of your mind like a bank account. You have a limited amount of available resources. If you make more withdrawals than deposits you will eventually run out of money. Similarly, if you throw yourself into your work and do not make allowances for breaks and time off you could find yourself depleted, physically and emotionally.

It is not just muscles and joints that ache when the body is overworked. The brain is prone to fatigue, too. Research has found that mental fatigue can set in after as little as three hours of continuous time on a task. Scientists recommend taking breaks every 90 minutes to combat this condition. Admitting the need to rest is not a sign of weakness. To the contrary, it is compatible with a commitment to becoming more productive.

Energy Sources for Recharging Batteries

Rather than looking to squeeze in more work (and draining more energy), how about carving out time to engage in renewal? It is possible to be more productive even if you log fewer work hours by making exercise and breaks part of your daily routine. Three opportunities for recharging can be found in different parts of the day and week:

- *Daily breaks.* Make time during the day for a short walk or a conversation with a friend. Whatever you do, try to not be part of the 50% of workers who say they eat lunch at their desk.

- *Home activities.* Look for ways to enjoy time once you get home. Turn a task like cooking a meal into a creative project. Plan a family game night to reconnect with your spouse and kids and allow yourself to have fun.

- *Off-day activities.* Unplug from your daily routine on off days so that they are just that- off days. Take a hike, travel for a mini vacation, or engage in a hobby. If you do these things, you will have less time for work.

If you struggle embracing any or all of these recharging activities, consider that renewal enables you to work when you are supposed to be working. In other words, we don't rest to be lazy; we rest to be more effective when working.

Ultimately, you are not paid for the number of hours you work. Rather, pay is based on value you create from problem solving and creativity. Both outputs can be boosted when recharging batteries becomes engrained in your daily activities.

Brand Builder

You are not a machine—relaxation is essential to restoring energy and resetting your mind to take on new challenges or projects. Too often, we worry that relaxation will be perceived as lack of focus. Keep in mind that relaxation is actually a commitment to boost focus! Work to become more adept at recharging your personal batteries by taking the following actions:

- Commit to engaging in a new or different recharging action for each of the three types (daily breaks, home activities, and off-day activities) in the next week. Identify obstacles to doing these recharging actions. What can you do to minimize or eliminate the obstacles?

27
Plan to Grow
Make Time for Review and Preparation

Personal growth does not happen by chance; it is the result of planning to reach the destination you desire. The CEO of a Fortune 500 company does not rise to the top of the organization because he kept showing up for work and getting promoted. Similarly, an Olympic champion does not pile up goal medals just because she trained rigorously. Yes, sustained effort is essential to improvement. However, the payoff of effort on results hinges on planning the outcomes to achieve and how to achieve them. Too often, we do not place high value on review and planning like we do other work activities. Do you plan to grow?

Energize Your Brand

Planning brings energy to your work and ultimately, to your brand. Author and success expert Brian Tracy says the key to personal strategic planning is to focus on return on energy, or ROE. It refers to focusing your talents and abilities on activities that will yield the highest payoff. Available time to create impact is limited- you have 168 hours a week regardless of your age, education level, or where you live. This fact-of-life limitation creates urgency to pinpoint the projects or activities upon which you will focus time.

Three practices essential to maximizing ROE on work are prioritizing projects, setting deadlines, and executing workflow. First, differentiating projects on the basis of priority should be a given in strategic planning. Even if projects have similar importance, they may have varying degrees of completion urgency.

Sometimes, urgency is dictated by the demands of others. Other times, urgency is determined by the potential impact of a completed project.

Second, set deadlines for project completion as well as intermediate steps to be completed to advance a project. Setting deadlines is effective for achieving goals because promising to deliver something to others motivates us to fulfill our promise. Have you ever noticed that you tend to get more done in the days leading up to a vacation? The deadline created by upcoming time off sets us into high gear to clear our plate of current obligations. When we have commitments to fulfill, whether to ourselves or others, greater accountability comes into play that spurs action.

Third, priorities and deadlines chart the course to getting work done, but unless the work actually gets done a great deal of time is wasted making plans. Working at a steady pace is a characteristic of productive people. Their workflow is steady, not frantic in trying to complete a task on deadline (although they set deadlines for themselves). They work more like the tortoise than the hare, plodding along with the finish line in view. They break down the end result into the tasks required to get there and schedule them accordingly.

Grow Time

Setting aside time to prepare for the upcoming week and reviewing the past week is one of the most effective time management practices you can adopt. Author and productivity expert Michael Hyatt finds a weekly review helpful. He sets aside time on Sunday evenings to go over the week just ended and prepare for the upcoming week.

Among the tasks he completes in his weekly review sessions are:

- *Determine next steps.* Review notes taken in meetings to capture follow ups, commitments made, and action items.

- *Follow up.* Go over previous week's calendar and complete any needed follow-ups (e.g., sending a thank you note, requesting a meeting).

- *Analyze results.* Review project lists to summarize what was accomplished this week and what needs to be done in the coming week.

- *Select next project.* Review waiting list of projects or ideas filed away for someday and move them to active projects if ready to be pursued.

A weekly review session of one to two hours is invaluable for implementing the three practices that maximize ROE: Prioritizing time, setting deadlines, and allocating time to achieve flow in doing work that stretches and fulfills us.

Brand Builder

You owe it to your brand to make personal strategic planning a priority. If nothing else, you will have an edge over others who do not practice prioritizing time, setting deadlines, and striving to get into a steady flow in their work.

Be intentional in your personal strategic planning efforts by doing the following:

- Conduct a weekly review session using the four steps below:
  - Select one goal you wish to focus on in the coming week (prioritize time)

- Lay out action steps required taking into account priority and length of time required to complete (set deadlines)

- Take action (focus on work flow)

- Review in an end-of-week session to go over results.

28
Pimp My Profile
Master Your LinkedIn Personal Brand Brochure

Whether you are a LinkedIn newbie or a long-time member, chances are your profile could use a makeover. It could be the needed updates are more like a tune-up than a complete overhaul. But, regardless of how much attention your LinkedIn account needs, make proactive management of your LinkedIn appearance a personal branding priority.

Your Self-Marketing Brochure

Your profile is the heart of your brand presence on LinkedIn. It is where users are directed when they click on your name. Many users equate their LinkedIn profile with their résumé. While profile contents include information found on a résumé, it is a much more in-depth platform for you to tell your story.

Moreover, a LinkedIn profile can be crafted to appeal to a certain audience. The information included and presentation likely differs for someone hoping to catch the eye of a corporate recruiter compared to someone wanting to attract potential clients. In other words, know the audience you wish to reach and write your profile accordingly.

Think of your LinkedIn profile as a brochure that communicates information about your brand. Imagine a print brochure for a company or product. What information does it contain? Background to educate and build trust, presentation of capabilities (i.e., features and benefits) to convey value, and a call to action such as calling a phone number or visiting a website that invites a response. If you dissect the parts of a LinkedIn profile you find that it serves essentially the same purpose as a traditional brochure.

Anatomy of a LinkedIn Profile

The stakes for creating a solid LinkedIn profile are high, too high to adequately cover all that you need to know here. However, certain parts of a LinkedIn profile rise above others in importance. Review four crucial elements of your profile- are you taking full advantage of their functionality?

- *Headline.* It is the "ad copy" under your name. You have 120 characters available to grab attention. You don't have to limit yourself to a straightforward title/organization headline. The headline is the first exposure someone has to your profile… make them want to read more!

- *Photo.* Keep in mind two considerations for a LinkedIn profile photo. First, include a photo! Users are much more likely to click a profile if the user has included a photo. Second, make sure it is a suitable photo. What is not suitable? Group pictures, you wearing a beer t-shirt and baseball cap, or a selfie.

- *Summary.* The greatest missed self-marketing opportunity on LinkedIn probably is a poorly crafted Summary. Why is it a missed opportunity? Two reasons can be cited. One reason is that many users fail to take advantage of the 2,000 characters allotted in this section. A second reason is the Summary is too often nothing more than a restatement of the résumé. Make use of the Summary section to write a narrative, a story about your professional journey. Save the lists of experience and skills for the appropriate sections later in the profile.

- *Experience*. You may feel that this section is easy to create as it resembles your résumé. However, look for opportunities to complement résumé-style text with images, video, presentations, documents, or any other material that communicates your capabilities. These multimedia components differentiate LinkedIn from a résumé.

Other sections of a LinkedIn profile include Publications, Honors and Awards, Skills and Recommendations, and Volunteering Experience. Review them periodically to ensure information is current. If headline, photo, summary, and experience sections are not interesting to the audience you wish to reach, people who view your profile may never see the latter sections.

Brand Builder

While best practices can be followed for creating a LinkedIn profile, you must ultimately write it in your own voice. Your profile reflects your brand, not someone else's take on what to say.

That said, learn by observing how effective LinkedIn profiles are constructed. Review these elements of your profile:

- Read headlines of LinkedIn profiles. Identify three headlines that you like. What characteristics of these headlines appeal to you? Rewrite your own headline, borrowing ideas from the three headlines you like.

- Review your LinkedIn profile Summary by first doing a character count (remember that you have 2,000 characters available for this section). How much available space do you have to work with when revising it? Next, review profile Summary sections and identify the Summary of three profiles you like or find interesting. What style or presentation elements can you adapt to your Summary? Finally, revise your Summary to work in elements from these other profiles.

29
Got MOOC?
Study with Elite Institutions for Free

One of the "if only" laments of unfulfilled potential relates to education. "I could have had better job opportunities if only I had been able to attend a better college instead of the local state school." Or, "I would love to switch careers if only I could afford the time and money required to acquire new skills." We can enumerate many reasons why we have not acquired the knowledge or skills that would enable us to achieve more. Our reasons are logical and convincing… at least to ourselves.

Today, the education barrier is being chipped away, if not demolished, by the availability of free courses offered by universities around the world. These courses are taught online, eliminating the distance barrier and expanding learning opportunities to a vast number of institutions. Sorry to shoot down some of the reasons you have for not adding to your skill set.

Breaking Down MOOC

The movement that is making available free college-level instruction is known as massive open online courses, or MOOCs. The current MOOC movement started in 2011 at Stanford University. In 2015, more than 35 million people enrolled in at least one course, nearly double the number of students from just one year earlier. Three top MOOC providers are Coursera (a consortium of more than 140 academic institutions and companies), edX (a partnership founded by Harvard and MIT), and Udacity.

So what exactly is a MOOC? The acronym stands for:

- *Massive.* It is not unusual for thousands of students to enroll in a course. The MOOC with the highest enrollment to date is "Learning to How to Learn" taught by two professors at University of California San Diego. More than 1.1 million people have enrolled in the course.

- *Open.* Not only are usually no restrictions on class size, but there are also no prerequisites for taking a course. And, they are open in terms of no cost to enroll (although some courses charge fees for a completion exam or certificate).

- *Online.* You are not confined to taking courses in a certain geographical area since courses are taught online. Study with professors at the world's most prestigious institutions from the comfort of your home.

- *Course.* The structure of a MOOC resembles a college course. Since MOOCs do not necessarily follow the traditional college schedule of fall, spring, and summer terms, more flexibility exists for taking courses when convenient for you. Also, many MOOC courses have shortened course length to fit the lifestyle of busy learners.

Whether you enroll in a single course or take a collection of courses that comprise a specialization such as web design or entrepreneurship, MOOCs enhance our formal education and training options like never before.

Education at Your Fingertips

Can 35 million people be wrong about MOOCs, or will your personal brand be positively impacted by investing time in taking courses? According to a study of Coursera MOOC students, the primary goal for enrollment relates to career benefits. Positioning for career growth or change is the top motivation for taking a MOOC course; 52% of students cited improving their current job or finding a new job as the primary reason for taking a course. Among those students seeking a career benefit, 87% reported realizing a positive outcome like a pay raise, promotion, or enhanced skills.

If you are unsure if MOOCs are for you, consider who is taking courses. Demographic data on Coursera students reveals more than 80% of them already have a two-year or four-year college degree. They have formal education but seek more to develop skills and strengthen their brand makeup. Chances are you will find some of your competition in MOOCs. If they are there, what are you waiting for?

Brand Builder

MOOCs stand to revolutionize how formal education is accessed and delivered. Intellectual resources of top universities are literally just a few clicks away. Explore how MOOCs can impact you by doing the following:

- Visit the web sites of the top three MOOC providers: Coursera, edX, and Udacity. Search their course catalogs to learn more about available courses and specializations.

- Do it! Select a MOOC, enroll in it, and take the course. And, finish it! Approximately 85% of enrollees who sign up for a course fail to finish. Set a goal to complete the course.

30

The Most Interesting Man (or Woman) in the World

Being Memorable is a Choice, not a Trait

Have you ever seen the most interesting man in the world? Perhaps not in real life, but there is a good chance you have seen him in television commercials. For 10 years, Does Equis beer was known in the United States for its "Most Interesting Man in the World" ad campaign. The commercials featured the exploits of a bearded, sophisticated gentleman who between his looks and feats lived up to the title of Most Interesting Man in the World.

How interesting was he? Some of his accolades included:

- "He lives vicariously through himself."

- "When he drives a car off the lot, it increases in value."

- "The police often question him just because they find him interesting."

After presenting a litany of the Most Interesting Man's feats, the announcer would conclude his bit in the commercial by saying "he *is* the Most Interesting Man in the World."

Why Interesting Matters

The long-running Dos Equis ad campaign created a mythical image of an interesting person. However, there is a useful takeaway from this fictional portrayal of interesting on an epic scale: Reflection on the question "what makes people interesting?"

This question is a must ask as you shape your personal brand. Let's face it- most brands are boring. And, most people don't seek out to buy boring. We are attracted to products (and by extension, ideas and people) that are interesting to us.

It is easy to understand the law of attraction in our role as consumer. The challenge is when we reverse roles and are the seller- how can we become more interesting to the people who come in contact with our brand?

Two Ways to Become Interesting

Being interesting is not a fixed condition. Avoid the temptation to think some people are more interesting than others... even though you would be correct to think that way. It is not a contradiction- being interesting is not a fixed condition any more than the size of your biceps or how fast you can run a mile. You can work at being interesting. Yes, some people are more interesting, but it is because of certain behaviors or practices in which they engage.

The good news is if you want to be more interesting, you can do something about it. But, you must make two commitments to succeed:

- *Put others first.* This commitment might seem counterintuitive at first glance. "I'm supposed to be working on me, so how does putting others first make *me* more interesting?" If you want to build trust and be liked (intertwined with being viewed as interesting), you must first show others you are interested in them.

  An effective way for putting others first is to ask questions to put others center stage with a focus on listening (see Chapter 21 "Listen Up"). Ironically, inviting people to play out the tendency of wanting to talk about ourselves has the effect of making *you* seem more interesting. Also, identify

positive characteristics of people you find interesting. What
practices can you borrow from others and apply in your interactions? Make others feel they are interesting while becoming more interesting yourself in their eyes at the same
time.

- *Work on yourself.* Complement the others first mindset with a
  commitment to making yourself more interesting. How do
  you do it? Just as with putting others first, there are multiple
  ways to work on becoming a person of interest. Begin by
  allowing yourself to have multiple interests. You won't always be able to enchant others with your knowledge of basketball, so be able to engage in conversation on a variety of
  topics.

  Also, strive to become a better storyteller. I am not suggesting creating fictional tales about your life. Rather, relate
  your obstacles, how you dealt with them, and what you
  learned from them by sharing in story form. Our stories define us, and they are likely more interesting than you realize.
  Third, be curious with almost a child-like view of the world.
  Ask questions, challenge assumptions, and stop taking for
  granted the world around you.

Not only will putting others first and working on yourself
potentially make you more interesting to others, you will enjoy a
more interesting life as a bonus.

Brand Builder

Interesting sells, but it must be authentic. You can't fake interesting! If you are a candidate to become the next Most Interesting Man (or Woman) in the World, congratulations. For the
rest of us, put the following suggestions to work for a more interesting brand:

- The next time you are interacting with other people (either one person or a group), practice putting others first by asking questions to learn more about them. Do NOT talk about yourself during this interaction unless asked questions. Focus on putting others first.

- Expand your interests by spending time with activities that you know little or nothing about. Do you find country music unappealing? Listen to a country radio station. Are you clueless about art? Visit an art museum. Step beyond your comfort zone and allow yourself to enjoy other activities.

31
First Things First

The Importance of Making a Good First Impression

You have heard the timeless advice "don't judge a book by its cover." When it comes to books, it is excellent advice. The information or entertainment value of a book may be better (or worse) than the tiny glimpse of a book's worth we glean from a quick scan of its cover.

In contrast, personal branding is very much about judging books by their cover. We make quick judgments about the people with whom we come into contact. Have you never met the person before? No problem- we still form beliefs about him or her in a matter of seconds. Psychologists say we form initial impressions after as little as four seconds' interaction. If that sounds fast, consider that people may make a complete judgment about you in as little as thirty seconds. We are cover readers extraordinaire.

Be a Cover Designer

The rush to judgment that is a first impression almost seems unfair. How can someone know the true you in in a matter of seconds? Years of triumphs, disappointments, challenges, and joys have gone into molding your story, yet they will "know" you in thirty seconds.

Don't hold the rapid pace of forming an impression against people you meet as it is our nature to categorize people and objects we encounter. It assists us in making on-the-spot judgments about the future value of forming a relationship with someone they just met. A positive evaluation makes us open to future interactions; a negative evaluation can lead us to avoid or limit future interactions with that person.

Two forces that make creating a strong first impression more challenging than ever, whether in business or in social settings are distraction and sameness. You may not be making a bad first impression; it could be that the people you wish to impress are too preoccupied to notice you. We live in an always-connected world in which a person's attention span can be as short as nine seconds. Thus, your first impression must capture attention. I am not suggesting resorting to attention-getting tactics such as altering your appearance, although how you look plays a major role in others' impression of you. I could dye my hair orange or wear polka dot blazers so people notice me, but if that is all someone knows about me, I have failed to communicate my brand's value.

Another pervasive challenge to creating a memorable first impression is sameness. Many businesses compete with other firms that make similar products, sold at similar prices through the same channels. It is almost as if you could take the logo off Product A, place it on Product B, and no one can tell the difference.

For your personal brand, be wary of the sameness that exists. Although a great deal of useful advice is given on how to build a distinctive personal brand, realize that if you implement the same advice read by thousands of others you run a risk of looking alike- creating sameness. Balance the benefits of following best practices with standing apart among your peers and competitors.

Manage Impressions

Another saying that has major implications for your brand is "you never get a second chance to make a first impression." If you relate this idea to the distraction challenge, you have precious few seconds in which to capture interest... if you are lucky enough that someone pays attention to you. Does your online presence reside on a slow-loading website? Forget it. Haven't posted to Twitter in eight months? They are on to someone else. Poor grammar or objectionable language used? No thank you. A bad first impression is not fatal, but do not be shocked if that second chance never happens.

So how can you make the most of the one opportunity to make a good first impression? Make sure you put these tactics into action:

- *Dress the part.* Clothing plays a major role in shaping people's judgments about you. The reason? Clothing covers more than 95% of your body. Know what clothing is normal and accepted for people with whom you aspire to associate or become.

- *Exhibit competence.* Listen to what the other person says or asks (notice that effective listening continues to pop up as a personal brand influence). Give a response that reflects understanding of what the person said.

- *Convey reliability.* Convince the other person that you there in the moment by focusing your attention on him or her. Only make promises to the person upon which you can deliver. Following through on your word can aid brand memorability; failure to follow through can do the same, albeit in an undesirable way.

Here is one more quote to consider: "You never have to make up for a good start." A positive, memorable first impression aligned with your brand's value proposition can gain attention and make second chances a moot point.

Brand Builder

Many personal branding experts view impression management as one of the most important tasks involved in managing your brand. First impressions are the basis for attitudes people have about you and what you offer (like, dislike, or indifferent). Be proactive in managing impressions you give off that shape how people perceive you.

Take charge of first impressions made by doing the following:

- Think about how sameness could be inhibiting your ability to make a memorable impression. How could you overcome the challenge of sameness and become more memorable through a) wardrobe choices and b) the messages you share on your social media accounts?

- Think about people with whom you have interacted recently, either in person or online. Select one person who made a positive first impression and another person who made a negative first impression. For the person who made a positive impression, what did he or she say or do that was memorable? For the person who made a negative impression, what could he or she have done differently to make a better initial impression?

32
To Tweet or not to Tweet?
Twitter is not Just About What's for Lunch

Facebook may be the social network of choice in terms of sheer number of users. Instagram and Snapchat attract younger users in particular with visual, customizable content. The popularity of these social networking sites has prompted some experts to predict the ultimate demise of another platform that struggles to find its sweet spot: Twitter.

Known for its 140-character maximum on messages (known as tweets), Twitter launched in 2006 with mobile communication in mind. It is the go to social network for real-time conversations and information on breaking news and current events. The significance of content of tweets ranges from pithy ("I had lasagna for lunch and it was delicious") to life-or-death matters ("A tornado just demolished every house on our block but we're OK"). Chances are your Twitter content will fall somewhere in between these extremes... and that's OK.

Despite challenges to grow an active user base in the face of competition from other social networking sites, Twitter is still a valuable channel for personal brand building. Twitter is a tool that supports two activities indispensable to personal branding-networking and learning.

Expand Your Network

While you may think of LinkedIn as the social network of choice for professional networking, consider Twitter a complementary channel for connecting with people and companies. Twitter, like other social networking sites, smashes geographic barriers to networking. And, there are a lot of people are on Twitter- more than 320 million, including 150 million active users. Unlike LinkedIn, reciprocation is not required to make a connection on LinkedIn. The default action allows you to follow a Twitter account simply by clicking "Follow."

The ease of connecting on Twitter is great, but it does little good if you are lost when it comes to finding people with whom to network. Once you find people, how do you use Twitter to build relationships with them? Many applications of Twitter for networking exist, but four of the most fruitful tactics are:

- *Follow users in same field or industry.* Twitter's powerful Advanced Search feature enables you to drill down your search to specific words, people, and geographic locations. Also, search hashtags related to your interests to discover users who tweet on topics you like. A hashtag directory like Twubs lets you search hashtags and see users tweeting relevant hashtags.

- *Participate in Twitter chats.* Meet new people and develop relationships with existing connections on Twitter chats. These are real-time discussions held on a regular schedule. Chats are started around shared interests. For example, the chat #blogchat is a weekly gathering of bloggers. Twubs also has a chat directory feature.

- *Retweet posts made by others.* A great way to get noticed by Twitter users is to share (called retweeting) their posts. Retweeting is positive reinforcement that is taken as a compliment. Also, it is a way that a person you retweet may come to know you.

- *Build segmented lists.* If the pace of tweets in your feed feel like water blasting from a fire hose, create order by building segmented lists. You can build lists based on industry (web design pros and agencies), interests (e.g., basket-ball) or geography (e.g., Atlanta area). Like retweets, add-ing users to a list acknowledges you find their content interesting and raises their awareness of you.

Like traditional networking, using Twitter to grow your pro-fessional network takes time. It is an ongoing process, not a one-time task.

Free Professional Development

How would you like to have access to some of the top minds and organizations in a profession or industry? How much would making connections cost? With Twitter, the cost is *zero*. Twitter has been called the world's best free professional development tool. A wealth of information and viewpoints is just a few clicks away.

Perhaps you have not thought of Twitter as a learning tool. After all, much of the content found on Twitter is not exactly thought provoking (think cat photos). Yet, Twitter offers many opportunities for professional development. Among the most popular uses of Twitter for learning are:

- *Talk to other people in your field.* The most obvious learning ben-efit is tapping your connections to gain knowledge.

- *Access long-form content such as articles and videos from links embed-ded in tweets.* You may be wondering how much can one learn from a 140-character message. Not too much, perhaps, but tweets often contain links to web sites, blog posts, video, or other forms of content.

- *Engage in focused, real-time conversations with Twitter chats.* The question-and-answer format used by many chats facilitates learning.

- *Filter content in your news feed to targeted topics by following hashtags.* Hashtags benefit you beyond finding new people to follow. Use hashtags to cut through the clutter your Twitter news feed can be in order to focus on subject-specific tweets.

- *Create segmented lists of users based on topic, local area, or other criterion.* In addition to networking benefits that comes when curating lists of users, accessing those lists gives you targeted content based on the commonality of users in the list.

Twitter complements other professional development methods; it does not replace them. It cannot facilitate deep learning like that experienced in a course or training program.

Brand Builder

Are you on Twitter? If not or if you are not an active user, you might wonder how spending time on yet another social networking site could help you. While results may vary when trying the networking and learning tips shared, many people conclude their personal brand benefits from their Twitter involvement. Conduct your own Twitter experiment by doing the following:

- Use a Twitter chat directory like Twubs to find a Twitter chat related to your interests. Attend the next three sessions of that chat (. Follow participants from the sessions if their professional background or interests are similar to yours.

- Segment your Twitter followers by constructing lists. If you have no lists, start small by setting up one list based on subject, industry, geographic area, or other relevant criterion. As you add followers, add them to one or more lists as appropriate. Create additional lists as you become more comfortable with the practice.

33
Kiss FEAR Goodbye
Act on the Source of Limitations

I hope the chapter title does not oversell. You will not receive a secret formula for casting off fear. In fact, dismissing all fear would be bad. For example, you need to be concerned about oncoming cars if you are standing in the crosswalk on a busy city street. Fear is an emotional response that has existed as long as people have walked the earth. It is a fight-or-flight reaction to a threat. If a hungry lion chased you, fear would be a most appropriate state.

Thankfully, we are not likely to find ourselves trying to stay a step ahead of a lion or any other animal that eyes us for lunch. Yet, fear stymies us daily, limiting our growth and happiness. Correction, it is not fear but rather FEAR The FEAR that is a source of limitation to personal growth is not the natural reaction to a credible threat. Instead, it is an irrational response to a non-existent obstacle. Perhaps you have heard of this FEAR before. It is an acrostic meaning:

False
Evidence
Appearing
Real

While we often invest great effort in rationalizing FEAR, it is a potentially destructive force that threatens development of your brand.

Recognize FEAR

The decision to build your professional identity and career like a brand manager will draw naysayers, critics, and doubters. Surprisingly, their voices can be channeled through a single person... the one you see in the mirror. We can self-sabotage our growth before taking even the smallest of steps forward. How do we manage to interfere with the pursuit of happiness? One way is through presenting false evidence that when accepted leads to a poor self-image. We tell ourselves we could not possibly achieve success of a senior director, salesperson of the year, or honor graduate. Along the way, we have convinced ourselves that we lack the intelligence, interpersonal skills, or connections to achieve more.

Another source of false evidence comes from comparing ourselves to others. We see ourselves incapable of achieving what others who have already arrived at where we want to be, conveniently overlooking the struggles, setbacks, and adversity they faced. Whether the false evidence comes from misreading ourselves or others around us, the result is the same: Limiting our growth opportunities.

FEAR need not be the culprit responsible for the lament "what might have been." Although FEAR and fear are actually two different things (one imagined and one legitimate), we tend to see them as one and the same. Thus, treating FEAR like fear is appropriate. A vital step in dealing with fear is acknowledging the source. What is the root of the fear you feel? A common source of fear is past experience. If you are afraid of being in the water, it may be because of an unpleasant experience you had as a child. Or, it may not be something that happened to you at all; the bad experience of someone else could be the source of your fear. In either case, fear may be rooted in flimsy recollections that are holding you back.

But, even when the evidence is false, if it appears real it is real until we are convinced otherwise. So, how do we sift through our beliefs, false or real, to recognize sources of fear? Self-reflection techniques like meditation or journaling can uncover fears that are obstacles to personal growth.

Confront FEAR

Recognizing FEAR and understanding its limiting effects on your brand is the starting point. However, staring down fears does little good without resolving to confront and destroy the false evidence inhibiting your growth. The antidote to fear is simple: Action. Doing something that negates the false evidence is the answer. However, we often lack the confidence to do battle with the false evidence. Action cures fear.

Once the source of fear is recognized, deal with fear by changing your vocabulary to encourage action. Transform feelings of fear expressed negatively to affirmations of positive thoughts or behaviors. For example, FEAR might be casting doubt on your suitability for a promotion in your current organization. Defeat the fear embedded in self-doubt by expressing in positive terms how to deal with the obstacle and state action(s) to take to act on the affirmative statement.

The sequence might go like this:

Fear: I am afraid I do not have the right qualifications for the job.

Affirmation: I can acquire the skills needed to meet qualifications for the job.

Action: I will search online for courses, videos, and books that can add to my knowledge base.

This example is not meant to suggest you can magically get whatever you want by saying the "right" things. But, you can envision someone getting ensnared in negative thoughts and going no further. In that case, we both know the likely answer of whether he gets the promotion.

Brand Builder

FEAR is one of the most destructive forces to your personal brand. We cannot blame our parents, boss, economy, technology, or any other force—FEAR is our own creation. Negate the limiting effects of FEAR by taking these two actions:

- Identify a fear that is negatively affecting your professional growth (it is not a question of do you have one, it is a matter of what is it). What is the source of the false evidence to which you have accepted? How is it hindering your growth?

- Take the fear identified and apply the fear-affirmation-action template to address how you can overcome the limiting thought. Review it regularly to remind yourself of the self-imposed limitation and more importantly, the course to follow to change your thinking and eliminate the fear through action.

34
Enroll in Podcast University
An Education Program Delivered to You

If you work and travel to and from your place of employment, I have a disheartening statistic. The average American worker commute is 26 minutes each way. So how much time does the average worker spend sitting behind the wheel or in a bus seat? It comes out to about 216 hours each year based on average commute time for a five-day workweek, fifty weeks a year. What could you accomplish with an extra 216 hours?

You cannot add more hours to your day, but you can be more efficient in how you spend your time. Legendary motivational speaker and author Zig Ziglar often talked about "Automobile University." The concept was to make use of time spent in your car more productively by listening to audio tapes for self-improvement. The payoff according to Ziglar was significant; spending 20 minutes a day over three years listening to tapes was the equivalent of two years of a college education.

Technology has evolved since Zig Ziglar pitched the idea of Automobile University. Today, your smartphone or audio player holds your education program. And, podcasts have emerged as a new medium for delivering content that informs and entertains. Self-directed learning is no longer limited to your car. Podcast University is an anytime, anywhere channel for strengthening your personal brand Makeup, specifically knowledge.

Podcast 101

If you are unfamiliar with podcasts, think of them as recorded audio programs (although some podcasts have a video format) that you can listen to on demand. Podcasts emerged as a content delivery platform due to the widespread adoption of portable audio players like the Apple iPod (hence the "pod" in podcast). In 2016, an Edison Research study found nearly 100 million Americans said they had listened to a podcast.

So who is listening to podcasts? The profile of podcast listeners suggests they are well educated and have above average incomes. Many American podcast listeners have a college degree (22%) or have completed some graduate school or hold a graduate degree (29%). The median household income of podcast listeners in the US is $63,000, which is $10,000 higher than the median income for the US population overall.

Listening to podcasts does not have a cause-and-effect relationship with education level or earn a higher income, but the associations between a commitment to learning through podcasts and education and income are too striking to write off as coincidences. Moreover, the impact of podcasts as a learning platform on personal brand development goes deeper than observed changes in education level or income.

Podcasts and WIIFM

If you are not among the millions who listen to podcasts or have not considered podcasts beneficial for your brand, let's address the timeless question- "what's in it for me?" It is a fair question to ask, one that has several compelling answers. Here are five reasons you should be downloading podcasts today:

1. *Intellect.* You cannot help but become smarter and more knowledgeable about the topics covered in podcasts to which you listen. You can find information or entertainment on just about any subject imaginable in podcast

format. I love listening to marketing podcasts, but I also listen to podcasts on sports, popular culture, and other topics unrelated to my work.

2. *Diversity.* Learn from podcasters whose experiences and viewpoints do not mirror yours. Hearing different perspectives in the voice of those holding those perspectives can evoke feelings of empathy you may not get if you were exposed to the same message in another format such as print.

3. *Intimacy.* You identify with a podcaster's voice and pick up on his or her emotions. It's as if the podcaster is speaking directly to you.

4. *Free.* There is no cost to acquire single episodes or subscribe to receive episodes as they are released. While podcasts are not replacements for books or other traditional information products, they are a budget friendly complement to formal learning.

5. *Convenience.* Listen to podcasts at a time that works for you. Exercising, mowing the lawn, or commuting to and from work offer pockets of time that could be filled with learning. You can binge-listen to several episodes of a favorite podcast or listen to a single episode again and again.

Like any other consumption choice, the decision whether to listen podcasts will be motivated by the perceived gain from doing so. The short answer to that consideration is "quite a lot potentially."

Brand Builder

Podcasts can be easily incorporated into your self-directed learning activities. The convenience of accessing podcasts and the variety of topics covered make them too valuable to dismiss for building the Makeup dimension of your personal brand.

Expand your exposure to podcasts whether you are a podcast newbie or long-time listener by doing the following:

- Search available options by going to popular sources like Apple iTunes, Stitcher, or Podcast Directory. Look through different categories and identify two podcasts, one related to professional development and one appealing to other interests, to which you are willing to listen on a trial basis.

- Download three episodes of the two podcasts you are willing to try (you can listen on a computer, tablet, smartphone, or download episodes to a portable audio player). After listening to the trial episodes, decide if you want to subscribe to receive more episodes. If not, search for another podcast... but do not give up on podcasts!

35
Groupthink
Leverage the Collective Power of LinkedIn Groups

Your profession entails more than a job; it influences how you see yourself and how you are seen by others. We act on the premium placed on our professional identity by identifying with an industry, job title, or other badge connected with the work we do. Becoming part of a collective like a trade association or professional group is a way to link our work with something bigger than ourselves. At the same time, group affiliation carries practical benefits such as expanding knowledge or skills that enhance brand Makeup or making connections that could lead to opportunities like landing a new client or a better job.

The idea of connecting with others in your field may conjure negative feelings of regret, longing, or disappointment. What triggers these responses? A sense that you cannot invest time or money that professional meeting involvement would require. Too bad those meetings cannot come to you... but wait, they can and do in the form of LinkedIn Groups. I hope you are already sold on the need to have a LinkedIn presence (Week 24) and to create a profile that is an effective marketing brochure for your brand (Week 28). If you are unfamiliar with LinkedIn Groups or are not participating in them, it is time to tap their collective wisdom and expand your network.

There's a Group for That

Whether you are new to LinkedIn or have been a member for some time, the Groups feature is the best source for meeting people and growing your professional network. LinkedIn

Groups form around particular interests, industry or professional organizations, alumni of a college, or former employees of a company. For example, someone interested in the concrete industry could join groups like American Concrete Institute, Concrete Producer Network, or others among the nearly 1,000 groups that appear when the term "concrete" is searched. If you find there are no groups that relate to your specific interest, there is nothing stopping *you* from starting a LinkedIn Group to build a network of people with shared interest.

Although you can belong to up to 100 groups on LinkedIn, differing opinions exist about the number of groups you should join. Should you join as many groups as possible to broaden your network, or should you instead focus on a small number of groups and be very active with them? Both views have positive points. You can follow either approach- the main point is to take advantage of LinkedIn Groups.

Get off the Sidelines and into Groups

Why should you join groups on LinkedIn? A typical group includes discussions of topics that relate to members' interests, promotes useful content, and posts jobs. Members use Groups to ask questions to learn more or to solve a problem, seek advice on how to handle specific job situations, or stimulate conversation about topics or trends affecting group members.

Some groups have open membership, meaning all you have to do is click "Join" and you are in. Other groups are closed and require that a group manager approve your request to join. This feature is good because it is the group manager's way of maintaining quality, granting group access only to those people whose interests genuinely match those of the group.

Being active in LinkedIn groups benefits you in three ways:

1. *Learning.* Reading discussions posted by group members gives you perspectives that can add to your knowledge of your field. The experiences of members are valuable in their own development, and you can benefit from the knowledge, successes, and failures they share.

2. *Prospecting.* Following discussions and other posts on a LinkedIn group can be beneficial in identifying individuals that stand out as thought leaders. Their expertise, insight, and understanding make them influential among their peers. Connecting with thought leaders in your field can be less daunting if you begin building a relationship with them through group interactions. Also, posting and commenting in groups gets you noticed and can drive traffic to your social media profiles, blog, or website.

3. *Networking.* Last but not least, use LinkedIn Groups to add connections to your network. When you have group membership in common with someone else, it serves as a filter of identifying potential additions to your network and is common ground upon which you can make a connection request.

Remember, while there are more than two million different groups on LinkedIn, it is still possible that you might not find one that serves a certain niche or interest that you have. The good news is if a group does not exist, someone can start it: You!

Brand Builder

Like every other brand-building practice described in *New Brand Year*, establishing a presence on LinkedIn Groups takes time. Clicking a button to join a group takes only seconds, but as with branding in general, your work is never done. To get benefit from group memberships, you must consistently spend time engaging group members and contributing to the community.

Take the following steps to enrich your experience with LinkedIn Groups:

- Search for groups related to your interests. If you are unfamiliar with how to find groups, type a keyword in the search bar at the top of your LinkedIn page and select "Groups" from the drop-down menu to the left of the search bar. Identify three groups that interest you. Click "Join" (if it is a closed group you will have to be approved by a group manager- if it is an open group you are in the group immediately). You can receive a daily digest of group activity sent to your email inbox by setting delivery frequency to daily.

- Follow the activity of these three groups daily for one week by reading discussions, commenting, or even starting a new discussion. Observe the people who are posting and commenting in a group- what are their job titles? What companies employ them? Your interactions with a group serve dual purpose of offering your value to the community while enriching your network of contacts by adding people who add value to you.

36
Keep the Plates Spinning
Stay in Touch with People in Your Network

Growing up in a small town in Mississippi, there were not many entertainment options. So, when a carnival came to town, it was a must-see event. I will never forget the first time I saw a plate spinner in action. You know this person- he or she stands a thin rod on the ground, using it to balance a spinning plate... make that a bunch of spinning plates. The spinner begins by spinning a single plate. Once the plate is zipping around quickly in a tight rotation, the performer launches a second one. The step is repeated until several plates are spinning at once.

A challenge arises as the plates lose momentum and begin to spin slowly, eventually wobbling and in danger of falling off the stick and smashing on the ground. The performer focuses on keeping all plates spinning, giving wobbly plates needed attention to resume a picture perfect spin. If the performer gets distracted or is overwhelmed, one or more plates will crash and become little pieces. The performer's success depends on the attention to detail in keeping plates spinning regardless of how long they have been going.

The task of managing your professional network is much like the work of the plate spinner. Effective networking requires you keep the plates spinning, or should I say keep in touch with contacts. If not, the plates (contacts) will wobble and possibly fall away. You can be a star plate spinner by embracing two priorities in your networking efforts: Segment your contacts and adopt a touch system.

Carve Your Network

Building a network of contacts gets so much attention that we overlook the work of maintaining and strengthening relationships. We may not ask the question aloud, but once we meet someone at an event or connect on LinkedIn, answering "now what?" should be the next step. Too often, the result is little more than an addition to our stack of business cards or an email notification of a new connection. Networking becomes a game that gives off a feeling you have added to a collection or garnered a notch on the belt. As daunting as network building is for many people, there is as much or more room for improvement to become better at managing our network.

Perhaps one reason managing your network appears to be an impossible task is that it is... if you think of your network of contacts as one large cluster of people. You may have a network, but within that single network are different groups or segments of contacts. Think about the basis of connection, for example. Your network could include:

- Family friends or acquaintances

- Classmates and fellow alumni

- Co-workers

- Customers or clients

- Industry contacts

- And many more

Connection segments not only give order to the list of people you know, it can help differentiate them based on their role in your professional success.

Create segments by constructing a connections database (creating a spreadsheet could be a valuable long-term investment in network management). Setting up a database of who you know and segmenting it in a meaningful way has dual purpose of summarizing key information (e.g., job title, email address, etc.) and grouping connections in order to better manage communications with them.

Segmenting your network offers benefits ranging from reminding yourself how you know someone to setting a frequency for making contact with a person. The latter benefit is important because not all connections have equal value or significance to your personal brand. You may like every person in your network, but that is not the same as realizing some people have more potential impact on you. That impact can take the form of a person helping you expand your network, buying products or services, or hiring you.

It's in the Touch

Developing a system for managing communication with your network is essential to effective networking. If you subscribe to the simple definition of networking as "building better relationships," your networking efforts should be planned and executed with that aim in mind. You cannot build better relationships with someone if you met eight months ago and not interacted since then.

I admit to having LinkedIn connections for whom I have no idea why we are connected. The person likely gave a "cold" LinkedIn connection invitation that I accepted (had I been practicing network segmentation when we connected they would be in my connections database). I cannot network with them effectively (i.e., build better relationships) because I do not know how I can help them.

I keep bringing up having a tracking system for your connections because it is valuable for guiding your outreach communications. Who should you be communicating with personally most often? Who else should you touch base with periodically? What contacts in your network do not warrant frequent touches?

One approach to answering these questions is to set up an "ABC Network" to manage personal contacts:

- *A connections.* Close friends, key clients, a mentor or mentee, and other persons with whom frequent communication is fulfilling to them and you. You can help them, and yes, they can help you. This group is most valuable to you. Thus, you should interact with them more than others in your network.

- *B connections.* People with whom occasional interaction is enjoyable or allows you to catch up with each other; classmates, ex-co-workers or bosses, and industry colleagues are some examples. The utility you offer these connections is less than A connections, so less frequent communication is needed.

- *C connections.* People with whom you are connected but may not have as much to offer as you do to A and B connections. You met C connections somewhere along the way- at a training event, convention, or social gathering. Communication may be no deeper than liking one of their social media posts occasionally or greeting them at an annual meeting. The connection may evolve into a stronger relationship one day or not.

Two things to keep in mind about segmenting your network. First, the guiding factor in what segment to place a connection is what you can do for him or her- not the other way around. The greater potential value you have to offer, the more important a connection is to you. Second, review your connections database periodically and move connections to a different group if the relationship has evolved. Relationships can bloom or fade over time; ensure your classification of connections reflects the current state of the relationship.

Brand Builder

As challenging as building a professional network can be, maintaining and growing it can be a greater obstacle. Making a connection does little good if the relationship is not cultivated. Your task is like that faced by the carnival performer- you must keep all of your plates (connections) spinning. Take these two actions to manage your professional network:

- Create a connections database of the people that comprise your professional network. This project could take a while, but at least get it started. As you compile the database, look for ways that you can segment your network to group connections with similar characteristics rather than having one huge connections list.

- Come up with a classification system in which you assign some value to each connection. The ABC Network approach is one way to classify connections, or you may use another classification scheme you prefer. What is important is that you use some method for differentiating the importance of connections in your network. Then, establish a communications plan so that you are pursuing the goal of building better relationships (e.g., "send an email to five A connections weekly" or "spend 15 minutes daily on social media interacting with A and B connections").

37
Help Wanted
Let Mentors be Your Guide

If you watch a new home construction project unfold, you will notice right away that it is not a one-person endeavor. A minimum of two people are working together at all times, and usually there are more workers playing a role in building the home. It is too big of an undertaking for one person to pull off. Not only is a solo home building project impractical, it is virtually impossible.

The building analogy has relevance to managing your personal brand. It is like a building project, with a huge difference being the work on building your brand is never completely finished. A shared characteristic between home building and brand building is the need for help. Although you do not need someone physically working beside you to complete your work, we benefit when someone works with us to ensure our construction project is on track. That someone is often a mentor.

A mentor is someone with more experience giving guidance and support to someone with less experience. Do not read into this definition that a mentor is only for someone who is in the early stages of his or her career. While you stand to benefit a great deal from a mentor as a young professional, a mentor can have significant impact on your personal brand regardless of your age, job title, or work experience.

The "Why" of Mentorship

You may liken a mentor's role to that of a coach, with images of someone who teaches, sometimes yells, and takes charge over you. Do not confuse the services offered by a professional or career coach with the relationship you build with a mentor. A coach typically is task oriented (e.g., learn a job or reach a goal); a mentor is relationship oriented. While a coach can help improve short-term performance, a mentor is in it for the long haul to guide your development.

A mentor's influence on a mentee varies, but three primary roles of a mentor include:

- *Leading.* A mentor has experience- literally "been there, done that"- from which you can see the road ahead through the eyes of someone who has already traveled on it. Experiences give a mentor a perspective to share with those who have not yet had similar experiences. How do you deal with a peer that does not contribute on projects? What do you do if you lose your largest client? Your mentor has likely faced those situations, too.

- *Educating.* Another way you benefit from a mentor's experience is enjoying access to his or her knowledge, including a network of contacts. An experienced person will have a solid grasp on hard and soft skills needed to excel in your field. Your mentor can pinpoint certain skills that you should develop or emphasize. Also, your mentor is a source of relationship knowledge. He or she has likely amassed a rich network of professional contacts. People in mentor roles benefited along the way from people who made introductions that expanded their network. It is now their turn to do the same for someone else.

- *Supporting.* In contrast to the notion that a coach is someone who pushes you in return for greater performance, a nurturing a professional relationship is the basis of a mentor's connection with you. A mentor is interested in your development first. In the spirit of development, a mentor is your very own sounding board. Discuss ideas and viewpoints with your mentor before taking them to larger audiences. Feedback you receive allows you to fine-tune your message before you ever attempt to "sell" it.

Having a mentor carry out roles of leading, educating, and supporting can be comforting; you are not alone on the journey that is your professional life when you have a mentor walking with you.

The "How" of Mentorship

The easy part of mentorship is convincing someone of the benefits of having a mentor in your corner. Finding the right mentor... not so easy. It is not easy for a few reasons. First the demand for mentors far exceeds supply if you subscribe to the idea that a mentor is beneficial regardless of career stage. Second, some people may feel seeking a mentor is a sign of weakness, that they cannot "figure it out" on their own. Do not let professional pride get in the way of opportunities to enrich your career through a relationship with a mentor. Third, even if you are sold on having a mentor, the task of finding the right person to mentor you might be overwhelming. If your employer has a mentorship program, you may be matched with a mentor. Otherwise, you are on your own to find someone to lead, educate, and support you.

Assuming a mentor does not show up at your door to guide you, make the following considerations as you seek out someone to take on that role:

- *Have a goal.* What professional goals have you set for which a mentor can be a valuable resource? You do not know who would be a good fit as a mentor until you know the outcomes you aspire to reach.

- *Don't ask.* This advice seems contradictory, if not downright crazy. But, it is not a good idea to ask someone to mentor you when he or she is unfamiliar with your work. Many successful business professionals receive mentorship requests from people whom they have never met. The relational intensity of a mentor-mentee arrangement is too great to make a mentor request to a stranger and expect it a favorable response. Facebook executive Sheryl Sandberg says instead of taking the view of "get a mentor and you will excel" the mindset should be "excel and you will get a mentor." Let your brand and work make the case that you are worthy of a prospective mentor's commitment to work with you.

- *Build relationships.* If it is unwise to ask someone who does not know you to be a mentor (and it is), you need to build relationships with people at different career stages that could lead to a mentor-mentee relationship one day. While you would not want to judge each person you meet as a future mentor, create a network of connections that includes people who could fulfill a mentor's roles of leading, educating, and supporting.

- *Market yourself.* Consider your interactions with other people an audition to be a mentee one day. Most mentors take on the role as a way to pay it forward. Chances are someone mentored them; now it is their turn to help mold someone else's career. Be the kind of person a mentor wants to guide- positive, energetic, and helpful to others.

- *Have more than one.* It is challenging to find one mentor, but you have permission to be mentored by more than one person. Your network is comprised of people with different strengths and perspectives from which you can benefit. It is a business relationship, not a marriage, so it is acceptable to be in more than one relationship.

Like other aspects of building your personal brand, mentorship is an ongoing process. Reaping the benefits of mentorship requires a commitment by you and the mentor. It is not merely crossing off an item on your To Do list.

Brand Builder

Can success and growth from building a powerful personal brand be achieved on your own? Possibly, but I would feel much more confident in my future if I enlisted the counsel of one or more experienced professionals as mentors.

Take the following actions toward mentorship by doing the following:

- Identify one or more goals you have set for yourself that could be positively impacted if you had a mentor's guidance. State the ways you believe a mentor could help you reach the goal (or goals).

- Review your professional network to find prospective mentors to help you reach the goal or goals identified previously. For each person, rate on a scale of 1 to 10 the probability he or she would mentor you if asked, with 1 being "very unlikely" and 10 being "very likely." If the person's rating is anything less than 10, reflect on what you can do to strengthen the relationship and increase the likelihood of attracting that person to be a mentor.

38
Coffee Break
Expand Your Network by Meeting New People

Requesting a face-to-face meeting is at the same time one of the scariest and most rewarding networking actions. These conflicting feelings can be particularly strong when the person with whom you want to meet is someone you do not know. You could avoid this potentially nerve-wracking situation by never going out on a limb and asking to meet with someone. The "safety" brought by this approach would be a life of missed opportunities to meet and get to know interesting people.

Legendary motivational speaker Charles "Tremendous" Jones powerfully summarized the importance of mastering the art of meeting people when he said, "you will be the same person in five years you are today except for the people you meet and the books you read." Simply put, making an effort to meet people is essential for growing your network.

Enriching your network potentially benefits your personal brand. You become better known, more people recognize your brand value, and new opportunities arise as people you meet introduce you to people in their networks. Let others have apprehension about meeting people; embrace the possibilities for creating new relationships and growing your brand.

Brew the Coffee

A common setting for meeting new people is over coffee. Just as you must allow time for coffee to brew before enjoying the taste, you must lay the groundwork for a new professional relationship to develop. The best advice for meeting someone new is "take it slow." If you want to meet someone who has a job that you aspire to have or works for a company that would be an ideal employer, avoid the temptation to ask for a meeting in your first communication. The chance that the person will agree to meet you goes up when you take time to nurture the relationship and make them feel important.

One way to establish a connection is to interact with the person on social media—like or comment on their posts, share their content with other people, and even share with them a link or other information you think is interesting. This approach is a must-do if you do not know the person you would like to meet.

You can shorten the process of meeting someone if you have something in common with the person. When reaching out to someone you have not met before, establish common bond such as school affiliation (e.g., "Mr. Jensen, I know you are an alumnus of Michigan State." I am currently a student at MSU and value the advice of alumni on how to build a career."). The common thread could be a mutual acquaintance, fans of the same sport team, or having the same hobby. Regardless of what it is, having a shared bond means you are no longer strangers.

Stay in touch following initial contact by striving to offer value to the other person- continue liking or commenting on their online content and sharing information such as links to articles that you believe would be of interest to them. The goal is to build trust to the point the other person does not have reservations about giving up time to meet with you when you eventually ask for a meeting.

Coffee Time

Congratulations! You have set the stage for a mutually beneficial relationship. Now, it is time for the big moment- your first meeting with the person you have been "courting" by email, social media, or phone. Fortunately, you control the meeting's outcome through two behaviors: Applying common sense and using common courtesy. Unfortunately, many people fail because they do not exercise one or both of these.

The success of an initial face-to-face meeting hinges on professional behaviors including:

- *Arriving on time.* Being late to a first meeting, regardless of the reason, does not make a first impression.

- *Offering to pay.* You should pay for coffee (or whatever you consume) if you requested the meeting. It is an inexpensive gesture of gratitude to the other person.

- *Having one specific ask.* Go into the meeting with a goal to gather information. The ask needs to be general (e.g., advice on what to put on a résumé that would make you an attractive candidate for an organization) rather than specific ("Can I list you as a reference?").

- *Ending on time.* If you asked for 20 minutes of the person's time, move to end meeting after 20 minutes. If other person does not want meeting to end, carry on.

One other common sense mistake to avoid: Failing to follow up after the meeting. Post-meeting communication keeps you in the other person's mind and separates you from others who do not take this step. Send the person a thank you message (an email or even handwritten note) and pledge to remain in touch... then do it! You do not want to be the person who gets what he wants from a meeting and does nothing to sustain the relationship.

Brand Builder

Take a step toward being a different person in five years by growing your network through meeting new people. Accept the following challenges to meet someone new:

- Identify a person you would like to meet in person through the people you follow online or from a recommendation by someone in your own network. "Brew the coffee" by establishing communication with the person through comments, likes, and shares of their content on social media.

- Reach out to the person you identified and request a coffee meeting (assuming coffee is agreeable to both of you). In your meeting request, be sure to emphasize a shared bond you might have such as a mutual acquaintance or online interactions. Avoid the four missteps that often arise in an initial meeting by arriving on time, offering to pay, having a specific ask in mind, and ending on time. Follow up after the meeting with a thank you message and continue to be of value to the person in your interactions with him or her.

39
Venture into Another World
Embrace the Benefits of Learning

Acquiring in-depth knowledge about your profession is thought to be essential to becoming an expert. Committing to learn all that you can about your field- tasks required to do the job, companies in the industry, trends shaping future direction, and more- is important. But, do not be lured into the belief that a deep dive into studying your profession is how to approach continuous learning.

Developing expertise in your field elevates your competence and makes you more knowledgeable. However, there is an unintended effect of a narrow focus that could hinder your development: Myopia. An intense study of one product or industry can lead you to overlook how that product or industry relates to the world around it.

The Two Brains

The left brain-right brain theory in cognitive psychology suggests certain tasks are dominated by either the left brain or right brain. Also, the theory contends that people tend to have a preference for left-brain or right-brain thinking. Left-brain thinkers prefer to be analytical, engage in logical thinking, and are objective. Right-brain thinkers are more thoughtful, rely on intuition, and are subjective.

Learning and processing tasks are divided between the two brains. Left-brain activity centers on language, numbers, and critical thinking. Right-brain abilities include expressing emotion, processing images, and creativity. You probably have a good idea if you are a left-brain or right-brain thinker. If you do not, ask someone close to you such as your spouse or friend-others can observe the tendencies associated with left brain-right brain theory.

Dual Thinking

Realizing that each side of your brain engages in specific activities is helpful as you commit to continuous learning. The first step toward expanding knowledge is to go beyond your own profession or industry. You must stay abreast of news and trends that directly relate to your job, of course. But, in order to expand your knowledge horizons you must push the boundaries of the topics, events, people, and organizations with which you are familiar.

How do you step outside your comfort zone to learn from sources that are unfamiliar to you? Use the left brain-right brain theory as a foundation for out-of-field study:

- *Left-brain thinkers.* Examine fields such as accounting, finance, engineering, information technology and physical sciences. What are the trends driving these fields? From which fields do left-brain driven professionals draw inspiration or are studying (just as you are doing)?

- *Right-brain thinkers.* Look to disciplines that are considered to rely on right-brain thinking to perform essential job tasks. Such disciplines include art, graphic design, music, and writing. How do top performers in these fields go about doing their jobs? In what ways do they interact with and observe the world around them to influence their work?

The importance of observing both types of thinkers cannot be overstated. Our tendency is to look to those persons who are most similar to us. We can relate to them and believe we because of role similarity we can learn more from them. Don't miss opportunities to learn from how the other half lives, err — thinks.

Brand Builder

Our education system, higher education in particular, promotes specialized or "silo" thinking. We tend to become specialists in a narrow subject matter range. The problem is that most jobs or professions do not operate in a vacuum. People and organizations are connected to other people and organizations, many of which are in fields outside of our comfort zone.

Venture into another world by doing the following:

- Recognize your dominant thinking style (left brain or right bran). Locate information sources (e.g., blogs, books, or websites) not in your own profession or industry but rely on a similar thinking style to yours. Read from these sources as often as daily or at least weekly to draw from experiences and trends in those fields. Reflect on how you can apply what you learn from like-thinkers to your personal growth.

- Find information sources related to a profession or industry for which the thinking style opposite of yours is of primary importance. Read from these sources daily or weekly, too, to understand and learn from different thinking styles. Some questions to ask as you read include: How do people solve problems? How do they perceive trends or challenges occurring around them? What practices from their daily routines can you apply to your own?

40
Wallflower No More
Get More from Attending Conferences

In the Introduction, I confided that while I am sharing a year's worth of personal branding tips, I approached writing the book as a collection of "notes to self." I need direction and inspiration to build and maintain my brand, and this note may be one of the most critical for my brand. As an introvert, I struggle with engaging in face-to-face networking at meetings and conferences. Like other facets of personal branding, fear (or more accurately FEAR as discussed in Chapter 36) has a way of gripping me. It casts doubt on the value I have to offer others and whether people would want to interact with me (also discussed in Chapter 22).

Despite my struggles with in-person networking, I enjoy meeting new people. I am often amazed at the interesting people around me. Sadly, I deny myself opportunities to be enriched when I shy away from engaging in conversation. One of the greatest challenges professionals face when dealing with shyness is how to make conversation with strangers at conferences.

The personal and professional benefits of networking are significant, as is the opportunity cost of not putting yourself "out there." The good news is you can become more skilled and confident at conversation in professional settings. If you don't want to be a wallflower at conferences (or worse, hiding in your hotel room), you can transform into the networker you want to be.

Start with Why

Before implementing tactics that make networking with strangers easier, it is useful to reflect on why you are in this setting. You registered to attend the conference not to subject yourself to the discomfort of networking... even if that is how you end up feeling. Three main reasons likely explain your presence at a conference:

1. *You want to learn.* A conference has a full program of presentations, panel discussions, or workshops that can enlighten you about your job, industry, or personal growth.

2. *You want to earn.* Many professional meetings bring together buyers and sellers. Meeting new people can plant seeds for a mutually beneficial business relationship that otherwise might not happen.

3. *You want to meet people.* The potential for achieving the first two attendance objectives can be enhanced by embracing the possibilities of meeting new people. You will strategically seek to make some contacts; others will happen by a chance meeting in an elevator or at a meal.

If you are hesitant to "work the room" when attending conferences, reminding yourself of the reasons why you should network can put you at ease.

Get in the Game

The three reasons for attending conferences (learn, earn, and meet) establish the "why" for networking. Now, it's time to think about the "how" of meeting new people. Put the following tips into action to make the process of conference networking easier for you:

- *Change your mindset.* View networking as beneficial for your career and not just something you should do.

- *Make a list.* Who would you would like to meet at the conference? Research the speakers and attendees in advance to know who will be there. Reach out to the people you wish to meet by email to introduce yourself and express an interest in meeting in-person at the conference.

- *Know what's in it for you.* When deciding which conference sessions to attend, consider whether a session helps you achieve a content goal (what you could learn from a session) or networking goal (who you could meet at the session). In some instances, spending an hour chatting with other attendees is a better use of time than attending a session that is marginally interesting.

- *Balance time between relationship maintenance and development.* Spend time catching up with people you know, but avoid spending all of your networking time at a conference with friends. You help yourself and your friends by carving out time to make new acquaintances.

- *Get noticed.* Certain wardrobe choices could make it easier for others to notice and remember you. Examples include a distinctive necktie, colorful socks, or a golf shirt with a logo of your alma mater.

- *Make time for yourself.* If you are an introvert, keeping a frantic pace of sessions, luncheons, and social gatherings can be exhausting. Give yourself permission to skip an event (but not too many events) to recharge.

As you do the dance that is conference networking, remember that you can your life can be enriched by the people you meet. If that notion does not do anything for you, take comfort in the fact that networking is not usually fatal.

Brand Builder

Whether you can put ideas from this chapter into action this week or must wait until the next meeting or conference you attend, resolve to get more from in-person networking by taking the following action:

- Set at least two learn-earn-meet goals to achieve at the next conference you attend. Make at least one of the goals relate to earn (creating business opportunities) or meet (expand your network) to force yourself to work on face-to-face networking. Then, follow through and enjoy the benefits of meeting new people.

41

Going Up

Summarize Your Brand in an Elevator Pitch

You have likely given a speech at some point in your life—in school, at a meeting, or some other setting. Whether you were terrified or at ease in the moment, you had the advantage of preparation. You planned the content and practiced delivery. Chances are you were ready... even if it was just ready to get it over.

Another situation is almost certain to arise for which you should prepare. You will meet someone and be put on the spot to summarize you—who you are, what you do, and why you are valuable. Oh, and you need to be able to check off those three points in a matter of seconds. Wouldn't it be nice to be prepared for that task? Crafting an elevator pitch prepares you for such an eventuality.

An elevator pitch is a concise statement of an idea or product... or personal brand. The need for an elevator pitch arises from having a small time window to communicate with someone, like the length of time you may spend with another person in an elevator (say 20-30 seconds).

Entrepreneurs craft an elevator pitch to grab the attention of investors in the hopes of attracting financial support for their business idea. Similarly, you may need to sell yourself to an executive in your organization, a prospective client, or a hiring manager. The opportunity may come unexpectedly, so craft your pitch now so it is ready when needed.

Warm Up

You might be thinking to yourself "I don't have any use for an elevator pitch. Heck, I rarely ride in an elevator!" Of course an elevator pitch has virtually nothing to do with an elevator, but you may still need convincing of the value of an elevator pitch for your brand. Consider these benefits:

- *It builds brand awareness.* People are more likely to remember meeting you if you have a distinctive presentation.

- *It positions your brand.* You control what people think about when they encounter you based on the content of your elevator pitch.

- *Most people don't have one.* The task of standing out becomes easier when you have a polished, consistently delivered personal brand overview.

- *It forces you to think about your brand's value proposition.* Putting your benefit into words can be tough for no other reason than it is not something we do regularly. You will sound more confident about your value when you are able to put it into words.

- *It can lead to business opportunities.* An elevator pitch is a commercial for your brand. It serves to inform, persuade, or remind, just as an advertisement does. You won't make the sale or get the job on the spot (so don't ask), but an elevator pitch sets the stage for advancing a relationship.

Think of an elevator pitch as a conversation starter. It prepares you to succinctly communicate your brand value if put on the spot.

Make the Pitch

Now that you are hopefully convinced that you need an elevator pitch, a logical next question is "how do I create an elevator pitch?" Most communication experts agree that the following elements should be included:

- *Benefit provided or problem solved.* Explain what you do by describing the problem you solve for others, now a description of your industry or products offered. Include mention of the target market you serve.

- *What's your why (Meaning)?* Stating purpose, passion or both lays out brand Meaning that drives you.

- *Communicate your unique selling proposition.* What is it that makes you unique and stand out from others who do similar work or offer similar services?

- *Engage with a question.* Follow up USP statement with a question that relates to how person addresses problem that you solve. For example, if you are a digital marketing specialist you might ask "Does your organization use video to reach customers and prospects?"

- *End with a call to action.* Tell the person what it is you are looking to accomplish (e.g., I want to work with marketing decision makers to help them better understand video is a cost effective marketing channel").

These content points can be incorporated into an elevator pitch. Then, you must work on delivery. You want to be conversational and not sound like you are reading a script. The aim of an elevator pitch is not to gain something from the other person now. It is the starting point for establishing a relationship.

A final point about developing an elevator pitch: You may need more than one. Why? As with any communication, its content is determined by the target audience. What you want to convey about yourself would be different if you are introducing yourself to your company's CEO versus a prospective client.

Brand Builder

It is time to take on the role of creative director for Brand You and write a commercial for your brand, an elevator pitch. You will need it sooner or later- whether it be tomorrow, next month, or next year.

Prepare an elevator pitch with the following elements:

- Your name

- Benefit provided or problem solved through value you offer.

- Statement of Meaning- Purpose or passion- and how it inspires your brand.

- Identify your unique selling proposition (USP).

- Ask a question related to your USP so that other person connects a problem he or she might have to a problem you solve.

- Call to action- end with an invitation to continue the conversation later (e.g., a follow-up meeting or connecting on LinkedIn).

Keep your elevator pitch to a maximum of 30 seconds. Practice it until you deliver it with ease. It's yours- be ready to use it!

42
Put the "Work" in Network
Nurture Relationships Now, Use Them Later

Your network of personal and professional connections is one of the most valuable assets you possess. Many people treat their network like some sort of collection, with the primary goal being to amass a large number of connections. Treating one's network like a baseball card collection might be a way many people can relate to the act of networking. The more networking effort made, the more connections acquired. While willingness to engage in networking is admired, the effort needs to focus on quality, not quantity, of relationships.

As I look at the word "network," I notice the word "work" within the word always gets my attention. Networking is hard work! It is hard work in that it requires ongoing activity with different levels of frequency and time commitment. Although networking can be draining and even intimidating, it beats the alternative of having an inadequate, weak network. The practice of networking has been likened to a man digging a well before he is thirsty. Why? If you wait to dig a well (network) until you have a need, you are unprepared. You need not be thirsty if you will commit to nurturing relationships, old and new, in your network.

Do the Work

One of the most challenging aspects of networking is knowing how to begin. What should you do? Where? When? Put the following priorities in place to take the mystery out of networking and give clarity to your efforts:

- *Begin by putting other people first.* You will have limited success at networking if it is focused on how you benefit. Be a good listener, engage with others (put away your phone), and most importantly, enjoy meeting people.

- *Participate in face-to-face networking opportunities.* Professional association meetings and community group meetings offer numerous occasions to mix and mingle with other attendees.

- *Maintain current profiles on social media accounts.* Posting updates and sharing useful content is a way of keeping the "Open" sign on to attract others to want to network with you.

- *Engage people in your network on social media.* Congratulate connections on a promotion, new job, birth or graduation of a child, or other professional or personal life events. People appreciate the recognition... even most of those who claim to not want it!

- *Prepare and practice an elevator pitch.* Be prepared to have an impromptu interaction with someone you meet. You never know who is going to cross paths with you.

- *Make yourself available to network with co-workers and other connections.* Schedule get-togethers with individuals or groups of people in your network by suggesting coffee or lunch meetings.

Notice that each of the six priorities shared has something in common: work. You have to actively engage in listening, talking, sharing, and so on to convey your value and attract others to you.

Remember What Networking Is

The work of networking is easier to accomplish when the purpose of networking is top-of-mind: build better relationships. You cannot strengthen relationships by adding someone as a LinkedIn connection, then have no interaction with the person for two years… until you really could use a recommendation from her. The recommendation ask is much easier and more natural if you have an actual human-to-human relationship with someone.

Keep in mind two guiding principles in your quest to build better relationships through networking:

- *Embrace the practice of "give to get."* When you focus on giving to others (sharing content, making introductions, giving recommendations, and more), your generosity will tend to come back to you from others in the form of similar actions on your behalf.

- *Have a goal.* Avoid going to networking events armed with a handful of business cards but no purpose. The goal is not to see how many people you can meet or cards you can hand out. Your goal might be to make three meaningful new connections. Or, it could be to be introduced to an elusive prospective client. The point is to have a specific goal set before attending an event to guide your efforts.

Remember, networking may make you nervous, but it is usually not fatal. Enjoy building better relationships and at the same time, strengthening your network of connections.

Brand Builder

Dig your well before you're thirsty—commit to consistently work on nurturing your network of connections. In order to become a more effective networker, do the following:

- Review the six priorities that represent primary tasks of networking. Rank the priority that is currently your greatest strength as "1," the priority that is your next greatest strength "2," and so on. For the two priorities with the lowest rankings (5 and 6), consider how you can take action to improve. Then, do the work!

43
Protect Your House
Proactive Reputation Management Pays Dividends

Of all the associations others can make with your professional and personal life, reputation is the one thing about you that "sticks." Your reputation outshines and outlasts any degrees earned, job titles held, awards won, or income earned. It is the personal brand asset that is most enduring.

We go to great lengths to protect tangible assets we own—homes, autos, and jewelry, to name a few. Yet, we often overlook the importance of protecting the one asset for which we cannot be reimbursed by an insurer—our standing in the minds of others. Proactive reputation management is not paranoia; it is a strategic effort to shape public perception about you. A personal branding mantra that resonates with me is "define your brand or it will be defined for you." The thought of the latter terrifies me. I want to have a say in how I am perceived. Reputation management gives that voice.

Personal Brand Insurance

You can think of reputation management as playing defense or playing offense. While either mindset works, an offensive posture is consistent with personal branding being about defining and communicating your value.

In a crowded field or category, your audience will likely view personal brands being in one of three categories: 1) positive, 2) neutral, or 3) negative. Having your brand perceived positively is the most desirable of the three, of course. Personal branding is a strategy for shifting brand perceptions from neutral to positive. But, what about when one's personal brand is viewed negatively? Reputation management tactics can be used to minimize damage and even shift perceptions.

Think of reputation management as personal brand insurance. You do it because you need the protection from unlikely disastrous occurrences. And, proactively managing your reputation gives peace of mind that comes with knowing you have protected a valuable asset. Buying insurance is not the only way you protect assets. You also care for them with regular maintenance or inspections to ensure they are working efficiently. Similarly, reputation management is like insurance in that you can strengthen and reinforce your asset (reputation), further protecting it from harm by taking small steps regularly.

Proactive Reputation Management

Today, a primary task in reputation management is monitoring and managing your digital footprint. In particular, social media creates a permanent record of misspelled words, rants, and regrettable photos. Yes, a permanent record in that a moment in which you exercise poor judgment is screen-captured. You might hit delete, but someone who found your post humorous, inflammatory, or offensive may have preserved it to share with the world.

Online reputation management is more than eliminating or suppressing negative content associated with you (i.e., playing defense). It entails putting forth a consistent, positive brand image through what you say and do online... an offensive strategy.

Play offense with personal brand reputation management by doing the following to monitor and manage your brand:

- *Search*. Start by searching yourself wherever you can— search engines (Google, Bing, etc.), social networking sites (Facebook, Twitter, and more), review websites, and discussion forums—anywhere that people talk about organizations and individuals in your field.

- *Manage the evidence.* Review posts and content you have made (plus content associated with you via tags). The photo from that epic party at the lake reminds you of the great time you had and the adult beverages you consumed. But, it might lead others to question your character and values. Is it fair? No, not always, but people will make judgments based on available evidence. Manage the evidence.

- *Revisit privacy.* Social networking sites allow you to set parameters on who can see what you post. Apply privacy settings in a manner consistent with how you use a social network. If Facebook is a place for you to communicate with friends, you would have greater privacy restrictions than someone who uses Facebook to maximize brand reach.

  For example, up until 2014, Facebook's default privacy setting was global— anyone can see your content (the default for accounts is now Friends only). If you have never reviewed your privacy settings on Facebook and other online communities, it will be worthwhile to check how much access the world has to your accounts.

- *Write the narrative.* Your online reputation is influenced by content created by you or about you. Control the tone and content of your brand message by creating content that projects the image you desire. And, do it consistently as search engines are favorable to fresh, relevant content.

- *Get help if needed.* In some cases, a person's online reputation is hurt by a single negative situation, misunderstanding, or even the malicious actions of another person. Online reputation management services are available. They cannot eliminate dings to your brand, but their expertise is in using techniques to suppress negative information and bring positive brand associations to the forefront.

Reputation management is an ongoing task. It does not require extensive time to do. Rather, like personal branding in general it something you are always mindful of and strive to refine.

Brand Builder

Reputation management is more than a reactive tactic used to address negative online information about you. Approach it as a proactive tactic that reduces the likelihood you will find yourself in a situation in which your reputation needs to be "managed." Make reputation management a priority by doing the following:

- Revisit the proactive reputation management tactics shared in the previous section. In particular, focus on search yourself, manage the evidence, and revisit privacy. Begin your reputation management "audit" by doing these three tasks. Clean up and adjust as needed.

- Then, move on to the step "write the narrative." What types of content have you been posting online? You're your content contribute to a positive brand reputation? Neutral? Negative? If neutral or negative, how could you change content posted to move your brand toward being perceived positively?

44

Put the "Person" in Personality

Let the Authentic You Come Through

In a sea of digital sameness—profiles, posts, lists, and visuals that look a lot alike—the need to stand out is greater than ever before. An unintended effect of methodical approaches to communication and brand messaging can be a loss of authenticity. Showing your personality and personal interests may be stifled if we are all business in our communication with each other.

Giving others a glimpse into your personality is vital for building trust and rapport. This benefit is particularly powerful for interactions that occur exclusively online. Those connections may not know you IRL (in real life). So, revealing your personality is a way to attract others to you and build deeper relationships.

Authority Is Not Enough

A surefire way to stand out in your field or even within your company is to develop a reputation as an expert. A go-to person who can provide answers or insight is a useful resource to have around… but not necessarily an interesting one. I'm not advocating style over substance, but rather substance with style. Complement competencies and skills with personality. Building authority can demonstrate your expertise, but you will win over people with a personality that attracts and evokes feelings of similarity between you and the audience.

How can you convey your personality, particularly to people with whom your interactions are solely online? First, remember that messages we post online tend to be accurate indicators of our personalities. Be intentional in what you post. The tone of your messages, coupled with subject matter, convey how you are to be perceived—serious, humorous, sarcastic, wise, or witty—whatever reflects your true personality.

Communicating Personality

It's one thing to get the idea you should express your personality in communications with others. It's quite a different matter of how to effectively show the real you. Fortunately, being you is not difficult; the challenge is allowing yourself to do so and not hide behind a façade that obscures your personality.

Three simple yet powerful tactics for expressing your personality include.

- *Draw from experience.* You do not need to try to make yourself interesting by making up stuff (nor should you). Relate who you are by speaking from personal experiences.

- *Allow yourself to be emotional.* Do not try to be serious and straightforward every time you speak or write (unless doing so reflects your true personality). Express your feelings as they undoubtedly have an influence on your work. Hiding or masking emotions is a disservice to your authenticity.

- *Be conversational.* Display your personality by acting like a person engaged in conversation with another person. Doing so will put you at ease with your audience, avoiding the urge to sound professional and formal at all times.

Remember the words of playwright Oscar Wilde, who famously said "Be yourself. Everyone else is taken."

Brand Builder

It is important for your personality to come out in your communications, both in-person and online. Yet, you may struggle with how to infuse personality traits into your interactions with others. To help gain clarity, do the following personality exercise.

Consider the following bi-polar adjectives as they describe you. Rate yourself using the seven-point scale by placing a mark on the line you believe represents you.

Personable   Formal

Spontaneous   Planned

Modern   Traditional

Fun   Serious

Cutting   Estab-
Edge   lished

- After completing the scales, did a pattern emerge about your personality? What can you learn from completing this exercise that could be applied to expressing your personality?

- If you feel the exercise yielded inconclusive results, ask some people who know you well to rate you on the same items. Do their ratings reinforce your self-evaluation?

45
An "Easy Button" for Publishing
LinkedIn Pulse Offers Built-In Platform, Audience

When it comes to creating content, the philosophical question "If a tree falls in the forest and no one is around to hear it, does it make a sound?" often comes to mind. In the context of content creation, if you write a blog post or other creative work and post to your own website, does it have appreciable reach (i.e., make a sound)? Many experts contend your writing or other creative works should not be driven by exposure received. And, there is a great deal of validity to that viewpoint. Creative expression can positively impact you whether a work is seen by two or two million people. That said, go beyond self-gratification from the creative process and explore an option for substantially increasing reach.

LinkedIn Pulse is a vehicle that can amplify your voice. Launched in 2010 as a news aggregation app, LinkedIn acquired Pulse in 2013 and transformed it into a publishing platform for users. While Pulse still is an aggregator of content published on LinkedIn, its primary value is reaching the social network's 450 million-plus users worldwide via a blog-style publishing feature. Today, any user can publish in the dense forest that is LinkedIn.

Pulse is Strong

Regardless of your experience level with LinkedIn Pulse, your personal brand stands to benefit from using it as a publication outlet for your writing. One viewpoint about publishing creative works online is that you should avoid "rented space" like a social networking site and focus on your own real estate

185

(i.e., a personal website). An online presence need not be an either-or decision. Owned space in the form of a personal website is your flag in the ground, so to speak. Complement that territory by reaching a different yet relevant audience using LinkedIn Pulse.

Consider these compelling reasons for using LinkedIn Pulse to publish your writing:

- *A large audience.* LinkedIn provides a built-in audience with more than 450 million users worldwide. No individual blogger can approach the massive reach of LinkedIn.

- *A targeted* audience. Not only does LinkedIn have a large audience, it is a rather focused one. Users come to LinkedIn because of specific professional interests. They seek out people and content related to those interests. You can also target users by including tags that categorize posts' content.

- *Get found.* Pulse posts are indexed by search engines, meaning more people will find you through online searches if you are publishing content on LinkedIn Pulse.

- *Get noticed.* Publishing on LinkedIn can widen your audience as people outside your network will also see your posts. This added exposure could lead to new connections and even business opportunities.

Remember, you are not just creating written content—you are putting your talents on display. Pulse posts give others a glimpse of your knowledge and personality.

Best Practices

Hopefully, you are convinced publishing on LinkedIn Pulse could give a personal brand boost. But, if you have not used Pulse before as a writer or even a reader, you may have no clue where to begin. Start by keeping in mind these tactics:

- *Let passion inspire.* A natural first question about publishing on Pulse is what to write about. The answer is simple—share on topics or issues about which you care deeply. It makes writing less of a chore and more a labor of love.

- *Quality over quantity.* Resist an urge to publish frequently under the belief of more is better. Write when there is benefit to be realized, either for you personally or by sharing with others. But, do not fixate on posting x times weekly or monthly.

- *Go long.* Long-form content performs well. Posts upward of 2,000 words do the best for post views. That said, more than 75% of posts have fewer than 1,000 words.

- *Write a headline that captivates.* Headlines written to set up How To or list articles perform better in terms of views than posts with headlines posed as questions.

- *Be visual.* Include a visual in your post, specifically images. Although LinkedIn supports other multimedia content (e.g., YouTube video or SlideShare presentation), research shows views are lower for posts with multimedia content.

- *Push it out.* Share link to Pulse posts as a LinkedIn update. Similarly, extend the reach of a post by including a link to it in posts on Facebook, Twitter, or other relevant social media where you have a presence.

While there is not universal agreement on these recommended best practices, they give you a helpful starting point to try LinkedIn Pulse as a communication channel for your brand.

Brand Builder

- Publish a post on LinkedIn Pulse. If you have published before, you are familiar with the user interface and the process. If you are a first-time publisher, this exercise will acquaint you with the platform. To get started, log in and click "Write an Article" found at the top of the page just below your profile photo/headline and just above your news feed.

- Apply the best practices shared in the previous section as a guide in selecting a topic and crafting a post. Follow through after posting by pushing out links to the post on LinkedIn and other social media sites you use. Then, observe feedback on your post in the form of views, likes, comments, and shares.

46
#SeeAndBeSeen
Use Hashtags for More Effective Social Media Communication

One of the most helpful friends you will find online is young, less than 10 years old. Yet, despite his youthfulness, he is amazing at helping people find what they are looking for. This friend is not a person, but a hashtag. You know, the symbol that pre-social media went by the moniker "pound sign." That same symbol, which could pass for the twin of a tic-tac-toe board, is a valuable tool for sorting and targeting information online.

Hashtags came onto the online communication scene in 2009. Twitter was the first social networking site to incorporate hashtags into the user experience. Instagram, Facebook, and Google+ followed suit, linking hashtags in posts so that users could click to access more content on a hashtag's topic. Hashtags are shortcuts to organizing the vast amount of information online. On top of the convenience hashtags offer, they can be used as a device to get noticed by others. In short, hashtags serve dual purposes of enabling you to see and be seen.

Hashtags as Filters

The sheer volume of information available online can be overwhelming. Avoidance can be a defensive posture taken to not have to wade through content in the pursuit of useful, relevant information. Unfortunately, avoidance has a down side—you could be missing opportunities to meet and learn from brilliant people.

Hashtags can bring order to the chaos that is online communication. Use hashtags as filters to pinpoint content that interests

189

you most. Conducting hashtag searches on sites like Twitter and Instagram let you tap into a hallmark trait of the user experience on those networks.

Hashtags channel topic-specific content (as identified by a hashtag), saving you the effort of searching for content. For example, if you want to learn about leadership, the Twitter hashtag #leadership will return several hundred tweets per hour on average. That figure may sound like a lot, but compare it to the more than 20 million tweets an hour posted to Twitter. Now, hundreds of tweets grouped via a hashtag seems more manageable.

How do you use hashtags to see? Three tips to get you started include:

- *Trial and error.* Treat hashtags like search tools… because they are. Enter hashtags in the search feature on a social networking site. And, be sure to search hashtags in search engines like Google as they return content when searched. This method is hit or miss in that some hashtags will be a good fit for you and others not so much.

- *Observe others.* Who are people that you admire or find yourself learning from? Watch how these people incorporate hashtags into their messages. Explore the hashtags they use and follow ones that deliver value to you.

- *Hashtag research.* Many websites exist that allow you to gain insight into hashtag usage online. Two resources worth a look are Hashtagify and Hashtags.org. Sites like these give a glimpse into how a given hashtag is used by providing statistical data and showing content featuring the hashtag.

You can help bring order to your online experience by using hashtags. At the same time, marking outbound messages with hashtags can help others bring order to their online experience, too.

Hashtags as Signals

If you have yet to embrace hashtags as an online message element, consider the potential hashtags have for enhancing your personal brand. For example, when you use hashtags relevant to your field in your posts you help others find content that interests them. At the same time, you can become known as someone who shares or creates informative or entertaining content.

Another way hashtags are a branding tool is by spreading influence. Create your own hashtags as appropriate. Identify content that fits a particular niche by adding a hashtag. When you create hashtags, it can encourage others to post similar content and categorize using your hashtag. When others adopt your original hashtags, it expands your influence by reaching a wider audience.

Make hashtags unique. A generic hashtag might not be the most detailed descriptor of your content. Think like a brand— explore opportunities for supporting expertise in a niche using a relevant hashtag. Returning to the #leadership example, the volume of content posted with a heavily used label like #leadership could lead to your content becoming unnoticed. A variation like #leadershiptips or #leaderquotes creates opportunities to post thematic content around the hashtag(s) incorporated into your messaging.

Whether you are a hashtag newbie or longtime user, follow these best practices to get the most out of sending signals using #:

- *Keep hashtags short.* A hashtag consisting of fewer characters will be easier to remember and use. Not only are long hashtags harder to remember, but they can be annoying, too. What you think is a clever hashtag could be met with eye rolling from others— don't do it (practice #doasisaynotasido).

- *Less is more.* Although the benefits of using hashtags are numerous, don't get carried away using them. Let quality rule over quantity when it comes to hashtags. Be sure they are relevant and help other users find your content.

- *Know how hashtags are used on a platform.* Common guidelines for using hashtags in Twitter, Facebook, and Google+ posts suggest using no more than three hashtags in a post. LinkedIn has integrated hashtags into the user experience again after not supporting hashtags for a period of a few years. Instagram is a special case as you can use up to 30 hashtags in an Instagram post.

- *Research before you use.* When deciding on a hashtag to use for tagging posts, check it out on hashtag directory sites like Hashtagify or Hashtag Dictionary. Doing research beforehand could spare you from using a hashtag that has different meanings depending on the audience or could even be misinterpreted.

Brand Builder

Use hashtags to see and be seen online. Put hashtags to work for your brand by trying the following to expand their impact:

- Identify a hashtag with which you are unfamiliar but has relevance to you. Discover it using one of the methods discussed previously (trial and error, observe others, or hashtag research). Follow the hashtag for a week, observing top influencers using the hashtag. Are you connected with them? Would you benefit from being connected with them? If yes, you know what to do—connect.

- Experiment with a niche hashtag you create that can be associated with you. Use the hashtag at least once a day in content you post. Consistent usage will help expand the reach and possibly adoption of the hashtag by others.

47
Practice Makes Perfect
Begin the Day with a Morning Ritual

The numbers remind us of the precious fixed resource that is time—365 days, 8,760 hours, 525,600 minutes. It's all the time anyone has in a year. You cannot add time, but you can make choices about how you spend available time.

Among the most crucial time management decisions is how to begin the day. The first hour or two you are awake can set the stage for a positive day, or it sends you in a downward spiral of negativity and stress. If you had a choice (and you do), which outcome do you want?

A morning ritual is hardly a new practice, but establishing a daily activity pattern helps us maintain focus amidst the distractions constantly around us. We can get sucked in to a whirlwind of emails, social media posts, text messages, and more in today's hyper-connected world. A morning ritual cannot block or eliminate competition for limited time, but it can give direction to how you allocate that valuable resource.

Why a Ritual?

You might associate the word ritual with formal practices, perhaps even having a spiritual connection. We are adopting a straightforward definition, calling a ritual a practice in which you do things in a given situation the same way each time. Specifically, the situation is how you begin your day.

Morning rituals are practiced by many successful people. Rituals can reduce anxiety, improve performance, or modify behavior. Of course, practicing a morning ritual does not ensure success or happiness, but a set pattern of activity is a trait exhibited by many people who achieve at a high level.

Benefits experienced when you establish a morning ritual can include:

- *Creating a rhythm for the day.* A standing set of actions removes uncertainty about what to do first and is oriented toward accomplishing tasks for your benefit. A word of caution, the rhythm set can be positive or negative. For some people, beginning the day by watching the morning news or reading work emails can elevate stress levels. Practice rituals that create positive energy.

- *Establishing control.* When you begin your day with a consistent pattern of activity, you have control over how time is spent. Instead of being in reaction mode from the moment you wake up, a morning ritual empowers you to choose how you allocate time to start the day. It can be very assuring to know exactly how the first 60-90 minutes of your day will go before it ever begins.

- *Enabling small step accomplishments.* You may have heard the advice about how to eat an elephant—one bite at a time. A morning ritual sets a "snacking pattern" in which you can make small gains on completing a project, learning a skill, or pursuing an interest.

By now, you may be wondering what people do for their morning rituals. The length of time and number of activities vary, but ritual elements often by ritual practitioners include:

- Exercise

- Meditate/pray

- Read

- Work on a side hustle (design, blogging, etc.)

- Creative activity (e.g., painting, playing music, writing)

- Eat (including hydration)

There is no one right way to do a morning ritual. Try different activities to hit on the right mix of nurturing spirit, mind, and body for you.

A Ritual for Rituals

In addition to coming up with a pattern or structure to a morning ritual, you must manage that time block just as you manage any other task in your day. Otherwise, you may find the time set aside begins to look like how other parts of the day go—randomly and with little control.

Make the most of a morning ritual by including these three practices:

- *Write it down.* A morning ritual actually should begin the night before. Write down one to three things that must be done the following day. Identifying tasks for the next day orients you to what must be done, wasting less time pondering what to do first, second, and so on. Keep to a small number of tasks on the list as a to-do list that is continuously not completed can be a source of stress.

- *Wake up earlier.* This practice could be a deal breaker for many people. But, rising earlier is an opportunity to get more done. And, if you live with other people it may be the only part of the day for a quiet, uninterrupted block of discretionary time. Set a daily wakeup time... and a daily bed time to ensure you get needed rest.

- *Get your mind right.* When your first waking moments include thoughts of gratitude, you adjust your frame of mind to deal with whatever may follow. Beginning the day being thankful creates focus on what is good or working well in your life.

A fourth practice many people incorporate into a morning ritual is completing a challenging, difficult task. Doing so clears it from your to-do list earlier in the day, creating feelings of relief and positive momentum. Or, as Mark Twain opined "eat a live frog first thing in the morning, and nothing worse will happen to you the rest of the day."

Brand Builder

You only get one start to a day. Make the most of that one chance by establishing a morning ritual. Its length and content is up to you depending on available time and what you desire to accomplish. The main idea is to do it in some form.

- Conduct a one-week experiment with a morning ritual. Set a time block that you can follow daily. Do not overload your ritual with too many activities for the time allotted. Create a ritual from the mix of six elements given earlier (exercise, mediate, etc.). After one week, adjust how you spend your time as you see fit. The aim is to continue the practice of a morning ritual; the experiment part of it is trying different ways to spend that time.

48
Find Your Voice
Let Brand Meaning and Makeup Show in Messaging

Today's communication environment is at the same time empowering and intimidating. It is empowering in that barriers to message distribution have been all but smashed. An internet connection and keyboard are about the only requirements to be heard. If you have something to say, say it. No approvals are needed from media gatekeepers. We all have platforms available to us to be heard.

Communication can be intimidating as we have distribution available to spread messages but may lack clarity on what we want to say or how to say it. Not only do we want to avoid coming across as incompetent or unknowledgeable, we should strive to communicate in a way that reinforces our brand. The most effective way to articulate your brand's Meaning and Makeup is through consistent messaging. Just as a hallmark of corporate and product brands is remarkable consistency in their communications, personal brand messaging should have the same look and feel.

A best practice used by brands to meticulously manage their voice is a style guide. Organizations that create style guides use them to train employees on how brand voice is to be maintained across a variety of channels and situations. One example of a thorough style guide is MailChimp, an email services provider. Its Voice & Tone guide gives direction to employees on creating written communication for more than 20 different channels (e.g., Twitter, Facebook, and blog) or situations (e.g., user successfully completing a task or a task failure).

You may not need to go to the lengths of creating style guide for your personal brand communications, but the emphasis given to brand voice is something that could bring clarity and consistency to your brand.

Establishing Voice

The Message dimension of a personal brand tells our story. We use Message to not only build awareness of who we are, but give others a glimpse into how we offer value. A blend of stories from our past, imparting knowledge, teaching, and sharing others' brand messages comprises brand Message. Solid development of Meaning and Makeup is less effective if the attention given to Message lags behind. Simply put, finding and using your voice is not optional; it is essential for a distinctive personal brand.

Voice is an outward expression of who you are. How do you establish voice?

- *Voice.* It is your brand personality described in an adjective. A few examples of brand personality include lively, positive, cynical, or professional. Recall that clarifying your brand's personality was the focus of "Put the 'Person' in Personality" (Week 44). Use the insight gained from reflecting on your personality to identify your brand's voice.

- *Tone.* It is a subset of your brand's voice. Tone adds specific flavor to your voice based on factors like audience, situation, and channel. A hallmark of a great brand is consistency. However, tone allows for some variation depending on variables like situation. If your brand is usually light-hearted and playful, for example, it is appropriate for messages to take on a serious tone in response to a situation like a natural disaster.

Voice and tone are complementary parts of your Message. Voice tends to be consistent, while tone varies depending on audience and situation. Remember, the aim of establishing voice is to let your personality shine through. We experience many different emotions in the course of our daily lives. It is acceptable (and expected) that your own brand reflects living on the emotional rollercoaster of life.

Choose a Voice

A trait of online communication that can be maddening is the suggestion of a cookie cutter approach to messaging. Directives like "Five essential parts of a blog post" or "Nine LinkedIn profile must haves" paint a picture of sameness across different online content. The differentiator that is not talked about as much is voice. You can follow best practices when it comes to form yet still stand out if you have a distinctive voice.

Great news—you have choices for choosing your brand's voice. You are not forced to adopt one set method or style. Voice should be a reflection of personality, as suggested earlier. To fine tune your brand voice, answer these three questions:

- *Who is your audience?* Message content and tone must resonate with the needs of the group with whom you are communicating.

- *What are you saying?* Your message has to hit a sweet spot of what is true about you and what matters to your audience.

- *What is your style?* Answers to the first two questions can guide choice of style. Blogging experts Mark Schaefer and Stanford Smith identified five different styles that can succeed in establishing brand voice: 1) dreamer, 2, storyteller, 3) teacher, 4) persuader, and 5) curator. Chances are one you would be comfortable with at least one of these five styles. The teacher style comes easily to me as an educator and is the style that shapes my brand voice.

For all of the sameness promoted through best practices (whether intentional or not), know that you definitely have freedom to choose *your* brand voice.

Brand Builder

Knowing your brand voice and allowing it to come through in your communication are musts for strengthening the Message dimension of your personal brand. Gain clarity on your brand voice by answering these questions:

- Who is your audience? Describe characteristics of the people with whom you communicate online.

- What do you want to say? Identify the types of content you deliver to your audience, focusing on what will benefit them, not you.

- What is your style? Reflect on the five brand voice styles (dreamer, storyteller, teacher, persuader, and curator). Select one of these styles and use that approach as you create messages (social media posts, blog entry, comments, etc.) this week.

49
Worth a Thousand Words
Use Images to Boost Appeal, Impact of Messages

The internet is a vast clearinghouse of advice for any topic imaginable. How do you sort out quality from kookiness? A quality indicator I use to judge the merits of online advice is repetition. A particular point or suggestion appearing frequently has more credence than those mentioned less often.

One recommendation for creating online messages for a website, blog, or social media account is nearly universal: complement text with images. Adding an image to online communication can enhance quality in the minds of your audience. Including an image in a message gives you another channel to convey meaning without using a single word.

Also, statistics reveal that audiences value messages that include images. A few evidence points:

- Message retention is significantly higher when an image is included. One study found a 10% retention rate after 72 hours for a message without an image versus 65% for a message that incorporated an image.

- Engagement rates with Facebook posts containing images are almost 40% higher than for text-only posts.

- Tweets containing images are 35% more likely to be retweeted.

Qualitative and quantitative evidence points to the benefits of a visual element in messages.

Choose Your Images

The decision to incorporate images into online messages requires a follow-up decision on which types of images to use. While photos might come to mind when thinking of adding an image to a message, they are but one type of image in the image toolbox. The list below identifies frequently used images based on type or context in which they appear:

- *Headline.* Begin a message with an image related to theme or content of the message. An image can lure readers to read on or at the very least signal to them what the message is about.

- *Personal photo.* A message about a person (whether you or someone else) is made more personable when the person being talked about can be visualized.

- *Infographic.* Combine image and message into one with an infographic. They can be added to your own website, posted to your social media accounts, and shared by others via social sharing, email, and posting to their websites.

- *Memes.* If you want to gain attention or inject humor into messages, memes are a simple visual tactic to use. Take care to use memes only if relevant to your message and that do not potentially turn off the audience.

- *Quotes.* A variation of memes, using images containing quotes or sayings can gain attention and impart a nugget of wisdom.

- *Animated GIFs.* These visuals are relatively easy to make and stand out from static images used in most messages.

- *Screenshot.* For messages in which you teach or explain something, use of screenshots can complement how-to text descriptions.

The above list of images is not comprehensive, but their frequent use suggests acceptance by audiences. They are a starting place for you to add style and impact to your messages.

Image Management

By now, you might be sold on the benefits of incorporating images into your messages. The payoffs of images is only realized when using common sense and common courtesy. Failure to exercise one or both of these can lead to images negatively affecting perceptions of your brand.

Using the best practices below will not only minimize risk of image use harming your brand, they can bring consistency to your messages (a trait all brands should strive to achieve):

- *Give credit.* The freedom to use others' images through a Creative Commons license or other permission is wonderful. It expands the possibilities for including images that you do not have to create. Give credit where credit is due and attribute the source of an image that is not yours. Attribution is a two-way street; if someone incorporated your work into theirs you should expect credit. Do the same for others from whom you borrow. And, don't use copyrighted material for which you do not have permission to use!

- *Know the lay of the land.* If you include images in content posted across different channels, be aware that a standard dimension size will not work. For example, each of the major social networking sites has its own minimum

requirements for dimension sizes. Research image requirements for a channel before posting to ensure images enhance, not detract from visitors' experience.

- *Have a purpose.* The statistics on increased views and engagement with content containing images may compel
you to add an image or two to a blog entry or social media post. But, strive to be strategic in how you incorporate images. They should relate to the message you are
delivering and not used merely for shock value.

- *Think 30% rule.* For messages with a combination of image and text, limit space taken up by an image to no more
than 30% of a message's total space requirements.

- *Show your personality.* Use of images in a message can be a
way to show your personality or style. If you see yourself
as a teacher, images that inform and educate are consistent with your teaching style. A personality that is humorous or irreverent can shine through when you use
images with a similar tone.

Proper image use can boost the quality of your online messages; improper use can get you sued. Strive to enjoy the former,
not deal with the latter.

Brand Builder

If online messages you create tend to be text-only, work on
adding more visuals into messages. For each image type mentioned (photo, meme, quotes, infographic, GIFs, and screenshots), make use of free online resources to find or create relevant images.

- Incorporate one type of image you have never used in
message creation before. Choice of image type should be
guided by the purpose an image would serve (e.g., a
meme could humorously make or reinforce a point).

50

The Last Mile

Build Trust and Distinction with Follow-Through

I enjoy playing basketball, often starting the day firing jump shots to get my blood flowing. It is part exercise, part therapy as I have no cares other than trying to put the ball through the hole.

Although I am no basketball expert, the morning shoot-arounds have led to some observations about what it takes to improve my accuracy hitting shots. Many things have to go right—jump a certain height off the floor, make sure the ball has a certain trajectory, and exert just the exact amount of force needed so that a shot is not too short or too long.

However, the one aspect of a jump shot that seems to be the greatest predictor of success is follow-through, completing the act of shooting the ball with the ball rolling off my fingertips with my arm aimed directly at the lip of the goal and ending with a downward motion in which my arm is still aligned with the goal.

Here is what I have learned about the effect of follow-through on accuracy. One of three outcomes occurs when taking a shot:

1. Follow-through mechanics are as needed and the ball sails through the goal. Or, if my mechanics are just slightly off I may miss the shot but because nearly every aspect came off as needed I am pleased with my effort and can accept the result.

2. Follow-through may be slightly off but the ball goes in the goal anyway due to a fortunate bounce. Sometimes it is better to be lucky than good, as they say.

3. Follow-through is bad. I can tell from the moment the ball leaves my hand the shot is not going in.

How is Your Follow-Through?

You may have never picked up a basketball in your life, but the art of follow-through is important to you, nonetheless. Your personal brand will be enhanced or eroded depending on how closely you pay attention to follow-through. Think of follow-through as the last mile of a journey. The effort expended to get to this point is negated without attention to completing the journey.

Three areas of personal growth are impacted by the attention you give to follow-through:

- *Follow through on you.* This focus on taking care of you is not a selfish, egotistical issue. Follow through on your well-being by getting enough sleep, maintaining a healthy lifestyle (which may or may not include basketball), and being a good steward of your body.

- *Follow through on plans.* Goal setting is vital for advancing your personal and professional existence. Most people do not set goals in the first place, and others have goals that are more like faint hopes. Witness how crowded health clubs and gyms are in January but return to normal in a few weeks' time as those New Year's resolutions to lose weight and exercise often are forgotten. In other words, we don't follow through on our goals, making it challenging or even impossible to reach them. Stick with your plans!

- *Follow through on relationships.* This area of personal growth depends on your efforts to connect and maintain mutually beneficial relationships with others. The act of thinking of someone is not a substitute for reaching out to interact, either face-to-face or online. Rapid follow-through can be a way to stand out from others in situations like a job interview and a networking event.

Going the Last Mile

Commit to planning the last mile just as you meticulously prepare your brand for success. We tend to associate follow-through with action. However, the first step in effective follow-through is deciding how to go about taking needed actions. For example, any meeting you lead should include stating the next steps to be taken to follow through on ideas and recommended actions.

It may seem simple, but one of the best follow-through strategies is Do What You Say You Will Do, or DWYSYWD (pronounced dwizzy-wid,). It is an easy yet effective way to build credibility and trust. Why? Too many people fail to follow through and do what they say they will do.

Scientific research into the effects of following through in physical activity like swing a golf club or throwing a baseball has found follow-through is not a separate step from preparation and motion. All steps come together to create a single action held in memory. Similarly, follow-through in our dealings with others should be viewed as part of the dance of personal relationships. It is not an after-the-fact activity; it's part of the fact!

Follow-through is delivering on a promise. Brands make implicit and explicit promises. Thus, following through on discussions, plans, and commitments is a tactic for strengthening your personal brand. You can become known for living your brand promise. Similarly, being lax in follow through will impact your brand promise... just not in a way that benefits you.

Brand Builder

It has been said that the last mile is a lonely place. Failure to follow through on plans and promises derails otherwise reputable brands and people. When you follow through, you stand to gain in terms of establishing credibility, building trust, and creating positive associations with your brand.

- Self-assess your performance in following through on plans, promises, and next steps in a process. Use a scale of 1 to 10 with 1 being "poor" and 10 being "outstanding." If your follow-through performance rating is 10, congratulations! If it is less than 10, identify areas of personal growth (you, plans, or relationships) in which you need to improve follow-through. Focus on improving follow-through over the next week. Watch for obstacles to follow-through and observe the source—is it someone or something else, or are you the barrier to follow-through?

51
Wash, Rinse, Repeat
Close the Brand Planning Loop with Review and Revision

It has been mentioned before but worth repeating that personal branding is an ongoing process, not a one-time project. In other words, managing your personal brand does not follow the slogan "set it and forget it." Well-formed plans lose their effectiveness if you do not hold yourself accountable to them and learn from pursuit of those plans.

As you read this chapter, you are nearing the end of a year's worth of ideas for creating a distinctive personal brand. You may have embraced some of the suggestions in the book and put them to work for yourself. At some point in time, you must evaluate progress made from plans made and actions taken. Then, close the loop on personal brand planning by building on findings of your self-evaluation and set goals for the next period (e.g., month, quarter, or year.).

What to Measure

One benefit of taking a strategic planning approach to managing your personal brand is it reduces uncertainty about how to utilize your time. Among the first chapters of *A New Brand Year* were "A Balanced Scorecard" (Chapter 4) and "Ready, Aim, Fire" (Chapter 5). The placement of those chapters consecutively near the beginning of the book was intentional. I could have shared 1,000 ideas for personal branding, but if they are not practiced in an effort to spur growth (i.e., achieve goals) you may be doing the equivalent of treading water.

Review Chapters 4 and 5 for guidance on how to begin the strategic planning process. Why do that now as you near the end of a year (assuming an annual planning cycle)? Because you must repeat the cycle for the next year, beginning with setting goals. Set goals in different areas of your life as discussed in Chapter 4. Your quality of life stands to be enriched if you set growth goals in different life areas, not just for your career or finances. Goal-setting mechanics are shared in Chapter 5 as you are encouraged to set SMART goals (specific, measurable, achievable, realistic, and time-bound). Goals missing one or more of the SMART traits can lack in self-accountability.

The good news is that improperly set goals will hurt only one person. The bad news? That person is you. Set the stage for performance review at the end of a planning cycle by properly setting goals up front.

How to Measure

Just as you must set aside time to set goals for a planning cycle, commit to making time for evaluation and review along the way and at the end of the cycle. Otherwise, you have no idea if you are progressing toward your goals. It would be like getting directions from your GPS at the beginning of a road trip from Los Angeles to Las Vegas and never looking at them. You could make it to Las Vegas, but that is one bet I would not accept! Goals provide direction to a destination. Checking our progress toward goals ensures you are moving closer to desired outcomes.

For me, evaluating performance against goals is tedious compared to the excitement coming out of setting goals. I have found it helps to break down measurement into shorter time periods. Reviewing performance toward goals more frequently not only makes the task less daunting, but it also makes it easier to adjust or change what I am doing if I am not making progress.

Consider the following options for self-evaluating performance:

- *Daily.* Comedian Jerry Seinfeld shared how he checks his progress toward a goal. To become a better comedian, Seinfeld said you have to write better jokes. And, to write better jokes, you have to write daily. The "Seinfeld Strategy" entails having a daily goal (e.g., writing jokes), then placing an X on a calendar each day that task is performed. When the task is done consistently, the "X"s on the calendar form a visual chain, and you must vow to not break the chain!

- *Weekly.* Create an accountability group that shares what was accomplished in the past week. Having such a group to whom you report can be motivational as no one wants to report nothing accomplished. Pick this group carefully as some people could resent what you want to be, do, or have as a result of achieving your goals. Be selective and pick only those people who will be supportive... and you do the same for them.

- *Monthly.* Carve time into your schedule for regular performance review. A monthly meeting with yourself to review what you accomplished, progress made toward goals, and orient yourself to the next month by stating goals is the equivalent of glancing at the GPS occasionally to ensure you are on course.

Brand Builder

While setting goals is a must for effective personal branding, evaluating performance is important, too. Failure to do measure along the way would be like driving with your eyes closed- ineffective, likely to create problems, and unclear where you end up.

- This week, try the Seinfeld Strategy to measure daily progress toward a goal. Do it beyond the coming week and see momentum build to continue making progress toward that goal.

- Consider how implementing the weekly and monthly performance review methods could help you with closing the planning cycle loop and keep you on track toward goals. Who are three people with whom you could join forces and create a weekly accountability group? Identify the people and make the pitch to them to start the group.

52
See It, Be It
Visualize the Brand You Want to Have

Congratulations! You made it to the end of a year's worth of ideas for building and strengthening your brand. Looking back at the 51 ideas shared so far, you probably enjoyed implementing some of them, winced at the prospect of trying others, and conveniently forgot about the ideas that may have pushed you just a little too far out of your comfort zone.

Regardless of your reaction to the thought of adopting the brand-building suggestions in *New Brand Year*, one response you probably had (whether you realized it or not) is visualization of an outcome. You saw yourself doing something for your brand that maybe you have never tried. Visualizing the result either reassured you to give it a try, or it could have made you uncomfortable. Either way, visualization had an impact.

How to See It

Enjoy the benefits of visualization by taking a page out of the playbook of elite athletes. They are known for practicing visualization. They see themselves in crucial game situations—at bat with the bases loaded in the bottom of the ninth inning in a tie game, at the free throw line with the game at stake, or raising the championship trophy after scoring the winning goal.

It is more than daydreaming; these athletes put themselves in all-important situations long before they actually experience them. But, when they find themselves needing to perform at a peak level in a high stakes moment, they are aided by the fact they have already been there, done that... at least in their mind.

215

Visualization is a technique you can refine and improve at doing. Three tactics for making visualization part of your growth planning process are be detailed, practice, and put it in writing.

- *Be detailed.* Visualization of achieving an outcome should look like a meticulously drawn picture, not a fuzzy dream. For example, an aspiring author could have a book title in mind, a mock-up of the book cover, imagine the book on sale in stores, see themselves giving talks at book signing events, and so on. The more detail you possess, the clearer the picture of what you want to be, do, or have.

- *Practice.* Visualizing an outcome one time or even infrequently lacks the clarity of visualizing on a regular basis. Perhaps you need a tangible reference. For example, if you have a wellness goal to lose weight you may have a swimsuit hanging in a visible place to remind you of the goal. One-time visualization is a dream; regularly seeing yourself achieve builds momentum to make it happen.

- *Put it in writing.* The role of goals in building a personal brand has been discussed at different points (Chapters, 4, 5, and 51 in particular) as essential for giving direction to your work and life. Visualization that is detailed and rehearsed regularly can be transformed from mental pictures to written commitments. We want to move from dreaming to doing; writing down what we visualize ourselves accomplishing can energize your as well as create self-accountability for how you spend time.

They Visualized Success

Entire books have been written that share how people have visualized success before it came their way. What follows are two examples from different fields in which the person took a creative approach to visualizing the future he wanted to have.

Best-selling author and motivational speaker Jack Canfield once took part in a fun way to chart the course of his personal brand. In 1986, Canfield attended a "Come as You Will Be" party. Attendees took on the role of who they would be in 1991. Canfield went as a best-selling author, even carrying with him reviews of his popular books yet to be written. Of course, Jack Canfield did go on to become a best-selling author. His *Chicken Soup for the Soul* franchise has sold more than 120 million copies worldwide. Canfield's status in the self-improvement space is no accident. He visualized the value he wanted to create for others, then he did the work to make it happen.

Actor Jim Carrey once wrote himself a check for $10 million and put it in his wallet. On the memo line he wrote "For acting services rendered." It was post-dated three years. That check was written before Jim Carrey ever starred in a movie. It was a visualization of where Carrey wanted his career to go, a reminder to himself of the personal brand he desired to build. In 1994, Carrey signed to appear in the movie "Dumb and Dumber" for $10 million just before the three-year anniversary of writing that post-dated check.

The success achieved by Jack Canfield and Jim Carrey is not due just to visualizing a desired outcome. They combined immense talent and intense work ethic to produce results. However, visualization framed the work that needed to be done to get to the intended destination.

Brand Builder

Resolve that visualization will be an asset to shape your personal brand by looking toward the future you want to have. It is interesting that we often embrace looking backward in time. A high school reunion is a great example. We go back in time for a short period and fondly recall good times and relationships from our youth. Taking the same approach to visualize the future can help chart the course for personal brand success long before we ever arrive.

- Visualize an outcome you would like to achieve. It can be related to any of the six types of goals listed in "A Balanced Scorecard" (Chapter 4). Over the next week, reinforce the vision of that outcome by using the three tactics shared in this chapter (be detailed, practice, and put it in writing). Doing so will put you on the path toward goal achievement!

About the Author
Donald P. Roy, Ph.D.

Donald P. (Don) Roy is professor of marketing at Middle Tennessee State University. Don has enjoyed a marketing career spanning over 30 years, even longer if you count his paper route in middle school.

After graduating from Mississippi State University with a degree in marketing, Don began his marketing career with stints in department store management and consumer packaged goods sales over a 10-year period. It was during this time that he became inspired for the next stage of his marketing career. While completing an MBA at Mississippi College, Don decided to follow in the footsteps of professors that influenced him during his graduate program and become a college professor. He graduated with a Ph.D. from the University of Memphis in 2000.

Preparing the next generation of marketing professionals motivated Don to become a professor, and he has relished the chance to train future marketers over the past two decades. He has received teaching awards from the Marketing Management Association (Master Teacher Award) and Middle Tennessee State University (Outstanding Teacher Award).

Don has merged two of his professional passions—branding and mentoring— in his research into personal branding. His expertise includes using online communication channels for personal branding. He has made numerous presentations on using LinkedIn and other social media for personal branding.

Don and his wife, Sara, live in Murfreesboro, Tennessee with their sons Chris, Sidney, and Ethan.

You can find Don online at http://donaldproy.com and on Twitter (@Don_Roy).

www.ingramcontent.com/pod-product-compliance
Lightning Source LLC
Chambersburg PA
CBHW061436180526
45170CB00004B/1432